Dictionary of Braille Music Signs   by Bettye Krolick

National Library Service
for the Blind and Physically Handicapped
Library of Congress
Washington, D.C. 20542   1979

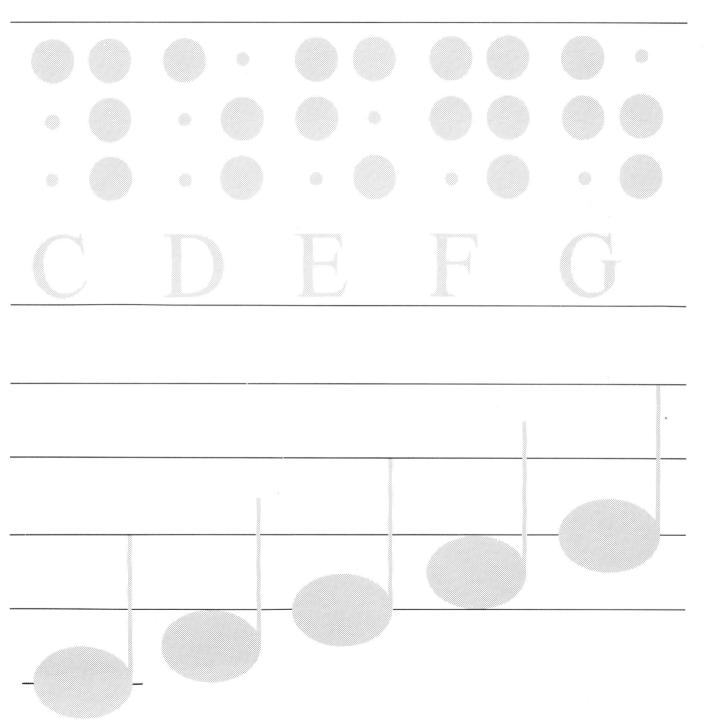

Library of Congress Cataloging in Publication Data

Krolick, Bettye.
    Dictionary of braille music signs.

    At head of title: National Library Service for the Blind and
Physically Handicapped, Library of Congress.

    Bibliography: p. 182-188
    Includes index.
    1. Braille music-notation. I. National Library Service
for the Blind and Physically Handicapped. II. Title.
MT38.K76   781'.24   78-21301
ISBN 0-8444-0277-X

TABLE OF CONTENTS

FOREWORD

The *Dictionary of Braille Music Signs* is designed to gather into a single resource definitions of braille music signs used since 1888 and to provide explanations of the wide variety of formats in which these signs have been used at different times by publishers around the world. More than 400 music signs and approximately 100 literary abbreviations are included. Since this is a dictionary of braille signs, not a dictionary of music, musical terms are not defined. For these, the reader is referred to the *Harvard Brief Dictionary of Music*, available in print and braille.

In addition to determining the meaning of braille music signs, the reader must understand the relationships established by literary braille abbreviations, the use of special braille devices not used in print, and the general format or arrangement of the signs on the braille page. To meet these needs, the volume has several explanatory sections supplementing the dictionary.

This book has been compiled primarily for braille readers by volunteer music braillist Bettye Krolick. Interested musicians and teachers of blind students will also find it a useful reference tool. Since it contains signs and formats no longer approved for use in the transcription of music, it should not be used as a transcription manual.

Frank Kurt Cylke, Director
National Library Service
for the Blind and Physically Handicapped

PREFACE

Research for this dictionary began at the Hayes Library of the Perkins School for the Blind, Watertown, Massachusetts, where it was my privilege to examine Louis Braille's 1829 publication proposing the use of a 6-dot cell with one code for the literary alphabet and another code for music. After studying this and other historical documents, I continued my research by reading countless selections of braille music and by studying every publication about braille music I could secure from sources in this country and abroad.

The Library of Congress's extensive collections of braille and print music were invaluable resources in determining meanings of braille signs. The braille collection also served as a basis for decisions about inclusion or exclusion of terms and formats.

This dictionary was suggested by Eyler Robert Coates, former head of the NLS Music Section. I would also like to express my appreciation for the valuable assistance given by Kenneth Stuckey, research librarian of the Perkins School; Georgia Griffith, braille music proofreader; Shirley Emanuel, Vicki Fitzpatrick, and the entire NLS Music staff; and Stephen Williams and the University of Illinois for providing the illustrations in the print edition. In addition, I am truly grateful to those people who loaned me personal materials, helped me locate resources, and read and commented on the manuscript at various stages of its development.

Bettye Krolick
Champaign, Illinois

In braille edition page xi

HISTORY OF THE BRAILLE MUSIC CODE

In 1829 the publication *Procédé pour Ecrire les Paroles, la Musique et la Plain-Chant au Moyen de Points* by Louis Braille (1809-1852) officially brought to the world the system of raised dot notation now in universal use. This document proposed a system of braille music characters as well as a braille alphabet. The alphabet was essentially the same as the one we know today, but the music code was completely revised by Braille during the next five years. By 1834, well before the braille system received official acceptance in France,[1] he had developed the basic notation of our present music code.

During this same period a number of other music notation systems were devised for the blind. Most used letters and numbers embossed in raised type, while some incorporated special shapes similar to the stems and flags of print notes. The main disadvantage of these systems was that they could not be written by a blind person.

Although Braille's music code gradually became the established system in France, no full printed explanation appeared in any language until 1871 when Dr. Armitage of

---

1. Authorities differ on the date of acceptance: 1844 (Roblin); 1847 (Rodenberg); 1852 (Watson), etc.

London obtained information from Paris and published *A Key to the Braille Alphabet and Musical Notation.* In 1879 an explanation was printed in German, and in 1885 a code was published in Paris. Since there were slight discrepancies among these three publications, an international music commission consisting of representatives from France, Germany, England, and Denmark, was formed to unify the braille music code for these countries.

Cologne Congress, 1888

An international congress with representatives from France, England, Germany, and Denmark met at Cologne in 1888 and accepted the report of the previously formed commission. The results of this conference, published in the respective countries, came to be known as the "Cologne" key.[2]

All of the following braille music signs have remained unchanged from 1888 to the present: signs for note names; rhythmic values; rests; accidentals; seven octave signs; intervals; triplets, sextelets, etc.; key signatures, time signatures;

---

2. A comparison of the English publications of 1871 and 1889 reveals that the word sign was changed from dot 1 to dots 3-4-5; the triplet (originally dots 1-3) became dots 2-3; and the double dot following a note or rest (originally dots 2-3) became dots 3, 3. Other changes did not involve specific music signs.

In braille edition pages xiv and xv

metronome markings; most of the nuances and ornaments, arpeggios; first and second endings; fermatas; fingerings and alternate fingerings; bowings; string signs; piano pedaling; print repeats; braille upper and lower-cell repeats; partial abbreviations; segnos; codas; parallel movement; the sequence abbreviation; the full-measure in-accord; the word sign; the repetition sign for vocal text; and the syllabic slur.

Rules for the use of octave signs were established as well as the principles of doubling and grouping. Intervals and in-accords were written to read down in music for treble instruments and in right-hand keyboard parts and up in music for lower-range instruments, organ pedal parts, and left-hand keyboard parts.

Among the few signs agreed upon in 1888 and changed or modified at a later conference were signs for the alternation of notes, the figured bass numerals, the tie, and the signs for fractioning (dividing a note into smaller values and reiterating it as sixteenths, a tremolo, or with other rhythmic values).

Paris Conference, 1929

During the next forty years basic signs remained as agreed upon, but new signs and formats were developed independently in different countries, several of which had braille embossing presses producing large quantities of braille music. Clef signs, for example, were not needed to read braille music, but blind teachers of sighted pupils requested them for teaching purposes. At least three different sets of clef signs were introduced and used by different countries between 1888 and 1929.

Because of his desire for again achieving uniformity in the music code, George L. Raverat, foreign secretary of American Braille Press (ABP) of Paris, volunteered in 1927 to act as liaison officer to bring together braille music notation authorities of Europe and America. "... after two years of unremitting labour, delicate negotiation, and constant travel throughout Europe and the United States, Mr. Raverat ... was able to announce that arrangements had been completed for an international Congress of Braille notation experts to meet in Paris in the spring, under the auspices of the American Braille Press."[3] The conference convened on April 22, 1929, with representatives from France, Italy, Great Britain, Germany, and the United States; nine other countries in Europe and South America indicated they would accept the decisions of this meeting.

The emphasis of this conference, by prior agreement, was on the standardization of individual music signs; any discussion of the comparative merits of formats was deferred. New signs agreed upon included the present form of the tie for single notes, the chord tie, the accumulating arpeggio, double whole notes, double whole rests, octave signs for notes below the first and above the seventh octaves, the phrasing slur, and stem signs. The adoption of symbols for

3. *Braille Music Notation* (Paris: American Braille Press, 1930), p. ii.

In braille edition pages xvii and xviii

clef signs, 8va indications, and print-page turns was the first official move towards facsimile transcription, giving blind people more information about print notation. Moving-note signs, alternatives for in-accords, were approved in 1929 but they are not an active part of the present code. The signs for alternation of notes or chords and for dividing a note or chord into repeated smaller values were expanded to include the prefixes for alternation and repetition in use today.

A general agreement of the conference was to continue the practice of writing chords to be read down for treble instruments and right-hand keyboard parts, but the United States decided to write all chords up. Therefore, music transcribed in the United States between 1929 and 1954 has the right-hand keyboard parts written up. Conferees were unable to reach agreement on figured bass notation, which continues to be an area for disagreement between countries.

Paris Conference, 1954

From 1949 to 1951 UNESCO aided international work on a unified code for literary braille. It then joined forces with the World Braille Council and the World Council for the Welfare of the Blind to sponsor more work on the unification of the music code. Louis Rodenberg of the United States coordinated plans and preparatory documents for the International Congress of Braille Music Notation held in Paris, July

22-29, 1954. Nineteen countries, including all of those represented in 1929, sent official delegates.[4]

At this conference significant strides were made toward uniformity of format as well as uniformity of signs. The majority of delegates officially approved the bar-over-bar format in which music is written in parallels, while a minority vigorously advocated the section-by-section or continental format written in paragraphs.[5] Other formats were officially rejected. The downward reading of intervals for right-hand parts was again considered and was agreed upon by all countries including the United States.

Another emphasis of this conference was the facsimile transcription of print music in every detail possible. Several new clef signs were added to the code, along with special signs for such facsimile details as grace-note slurs, square brackets above or below the staff, and any details added by the transcriber, such as rests to fill out one voice of an in-accord part.

H.V. Spanner of the United Kingdom was appointed to draft the report of the conference and to edit the new manual.

---

4. Official delegates, observers, and representatives of sponsoring organizations are listed in H.V. Spanner, comp. *Revised International Manual of Braille Music Notation, 1956.* Part 1. *Western Music* (Louisville: American Printing House for the Blind, 1961), p. v.

5. Personal correspondence with Harry J. Ditzler, official delegate from the United States.

In braille edition pages xix-xxi

The Spanner manual of 1956 includes a revised system of figured-bass notation and a new system of short-form scoring.

Since 1954

Since 1954 the braille system of music notation has continued to grow and be modified as needs arise. Canada and England have each formulated new systems for the short-form scoring of popular music. The *Revised International Manual of Braille Music Notation 1956: 1975 American Addendum* stresses clarity of transcription and de-emphasizes facsimile transcription. Some European countries have held meetings to discuss uniformity of signs and the section-by-section format as advocated by Dr. Alexander Reuss, a German delegate to the 1954 conference. Preliminary work is underway to develop braille notation for electronic, aleatory, and other new music.

HOW TO LOCATE A DEFINITION

The table of contents lists under the heading "Dictionary of Signs" the sixty-three braille characters in standard order. Multicell signs are listed under the first character and, within a section, are arranged in standard order by second, third, etc., characters. For example, in the section of signs beginning with ⠿ , the first character of ⠿⠿⠿ is listed in the table of contents as starting on page 90. The location of ⠿⠿⠿ within that section is determined by the second character ⠿ which follows the character ⠿ . ⠿⠿⠿ is located on page 95.

Definitions are arranged from the most common or current usage to the most unusual or oldest meaning. Each definition is in a separate paragraph and, where appropriate, is preceded by a guide phrase such as "in organ music" or "in pre-1929 transcriptions" included to facilitate location of a particular usage. Phrases such as "the preceding note" or "the following note" relate the sign to the note with which it should be associated. The word "immediately" is used to mean "with no intervening signs."

DICTIONARY OF SIGNS

⠒⠒   1. First finger on the preceding note or interval. A second fingering sign following immediately shows alternative fingering; two fingering signs separated by a slur show a change of fingering on one note. In some pre-1954 transcriptions with an interval doubling (page 175) in effect, two fingerings with no slur between indicate the fingering for the note and its doubled interval.

2. In organ pedal part: left toe on the preceding note or interval. A second foot sign following immediately shows alternative pedaling; a slur between two foot signs shows a change of toe or heel on one note. In early transcriptions, a doubled pedaling sign indicates the crossing of the foot in front; a tripled sign indicates the crossing of the foot behind.

3. In percussion music: left hand for preceding note. A right hand sign following immediately is an alternative.

4. In vocal music: syllabic slur necessary to the braille but not shown in print.

5. In margin: measure number one; if followed by dot 3, the braille measure on this line is incomplete.

6. In Spanner system of figured bass: print dash or continuation line; in braille this may be found after either a number sign or other figuration such as a number or accidental.

In braille edition pages 1 and 2   1

⠁⠁

7. In Rodenberg system of figured bass: indication that the preceding chord has the duration of a quarter note.

8. In neumatic notation: duration of the preceding note is doubled.

9. In pre-1929 transcriptions: first finger if other fingering is present; otherwise, quarter note rhythmic values; the preceding note or chord should be played as a series of reiterated quarter notes. If used twice and there appear to be too many beats in the measure, the notes should be alternated as quarters. See also definition 3 of ⠁⠁ , which is another form of the sign.

⠁⠁ 1. In the margin: measure number eleven.

2. In Spanner system of figured bass: two print dashes or continuation lines. It is also possible to have more than two dashes, each represented by dot 1.

3. In pre-1929 transcriptions: quarter note rhythmic values. This form of the sign is used when the music contains fingering; the preceding note or chord should be played as a series of reiterated quarter notes. If used twice and there appear to be too many beats in the measure, the notes should be alternated as quarters. In the following example, the first bar contains repeated quarter note chords, and the second bar contains alternating quarter note chords.

Example:

⠼⠙⠲ ⠸⠏⠴⠁⠁⠗⠌⠁⠁ ⠯⠴⠁⠁⠷⠌⠁⠁

⠆⠆ ⠆⠆   1. In keyboard music: first finger for the preceding note with the second fingering omitted in a passage of alternative fingerings.

2. In string music: first finger followed by a continuation line; the first finger remains on the string until the finger sign is repeated preceded by dot 6.

3. In choral music: abbreviation for the alto part.

4. In a keyboard passage played with alternating hands: when preceded by a space, the following notes should be played by the right hand; when followed by a word sign and a number in lower-cell position, the number shows how many notes are played by each hand beginning with the right. In the following example, the right hand is to play the first two notes, the left hand is to play the second two notes, and that pattern continues until ended by a hand sign.

Example:

When both hand signs appear and each is followed by a lower-cell number, an alternating pattern is established.
See   ⠆⠆ ⠆⠆ , definition 4, page 5.

⠆⠆ 1. Second finger on the preceding note or interval.
See   ⠆⠆ , definition 1, page 1.

2. In organ pedal part: left heel on the preceding note or interval. See ⠆⠆ , definition 2, page 1.

⠒⠒ ⠒⠒

3. In vocal music: two vowels are sung on the preceding note. In braille the corresponding syllables in the text are surrounded by quotation marks.

4. In margin: measure number two; when followed by dot 3, the braille measure on this line is incomplete.

5. When preceded and followed by a space: measure number two. Numbers without a numeral prefix may appear between measures.

6. In vertical score format for choral music: one voice separates into two parts; the sign comes between those two parts.

7. In Rodenberg system of figured bass: indication that the preceding chord has the value of an eighth note.

8. In pre-1929 transcriptions: second finger if other fingering is present. Otherwise, eighth note rhythmic values; the preceding note or chord should be played as a series of reiterated eighth notes. If used twice and there appear to be too many beats in the measure, the notes should be alternated as eighths.

9. In French transcriptions of neumatic notation: *distropha;* the preceding note is held for two pulses.

⠒⠒ ⠒⠒ In pre-1929 transcriptions: eighth note rhythmic values. This form of the sign is used when the music contains fingering; the preceding note or chord should be played as a series of reiterated eighth notes. If used twice and there appear to be too may beats in the measure, the notes should

4   *In braille edition pages 5 and 6*

be alternated as eighths. For an example, see ⠿ ⠿ , definition 3, page 2.

⠿ ⠿   In English chord-symbol system: the preceding note is played in the bass. The following example is a G major chord with B as the bass note.

Example: ⠿ ⠿ ⠿ ⠿ ⠿ ⠿

⠿ ⠿   1. In keyboard music: second finger for the preceding note with the second fingering omitted in a passage of alternative fingerings.

2. In string music: second finger followed by a continuation line; the second finger remains on the string until the finger sign is repeated preceded by dot 6.

3. In choral music: abbreviation for the bass part.

4. In a keyboard passage played with alternating hands: when preceded by a space, the following notes should be played by the left hand; when followed by a word sign and a number in lower-cell position, the number shows how many notes are played by each hand beginning with the left. If both hand signs appear and each is followed by a lower-cell number, an alternating pattern is established. In the following example the left hand plays one note, the right hand plays the next two notes, and that pattern continues until ended by a hand sign.

Example:

⠿ ⠿ ⠿

⠿ ⠿

In braille edition pages 6-8

⠿⠿⠿⠿

⠿⠿⠿⠿   In zither music: *Begleitungs Saiten* or accompanying strings; chords and intervals of this part read up.

⠿   1. Between two notes or chords: slur (braille term: simple slur); indicates phrasing in keyboard music, phrasing or bowing in instrumental music, and is the syllabic slur in vocal music. One syllable is sung on two or more slurred notes. If written twice in succession, the sign is doubled.

2. Between two fingerings: change of fingers on the preceding note.

3. Between two foot signs: change of feet; change to heel or toe.

4. In margin: measure number three.

5. When preceded and followed by a space: measure number three. Numbers without a numeral prefix may appear between measures.

⠿⠿⠿   Slur with a downward direction following a note; represents a jazz-type falling of pitch.

⠿⠿   1. Ornament; in print a V between two notes indicating a springer (*Nachschlag*). See definition 2.

2. Slur; indicates a half phrase. The print slur is bent into an angle at this point. Definition 1 applies to music transcribed according to the rules of H.V. Spanner. Definition 2 applies to music transcribed according to the rules of Alexander Reuss.

6   *In braille edition pages 8 and 9*

⠆ 1. C as an eighth, a 128th, or as a member of a braille rhythmic group. See grouping, page 178.

2. Eighth or 128th note with no specific pitch, as in metronome markings or percussion music.

3. In margin: measure number four.

4. In neumatic notation: C as an eighth note; the basic rhythmic unit or pulse.

5. When preceded and followed by a space: C as a double whole note. (Used rarely in some Italian transcriptions.) If numbers appear between other measures, this is number four.

⠆⠆⠆⠆ Metronome marking: eighth note equals dotted eighth note. The third element of a metronome marking is a rhythmic value or number.

⠆ 1. D as an eighth, a 128th, or as a member of a braille rhythmic group. See grouping, page 178.

2. In margin: measure number five.

3. In neumatic notation: D as an eighth note; the basic rhythmic unit or pulse.

4. When preceded and followed by a space: D as a double whole note. (Used rarely in some Italian transcriptions.) If numbers appear between other measures, this is number five.

⠆ 1. E as an eighth, a 128th, or as a member of a braille rhythmic group. See grouping, page 178.

2. In margin: measure number six.

⠒⠒ 3. In neumatic notation: E as an eighth note; the basic rhythmic unit or pulse.

4. When preceded and followed by a space: E as a double whole note. (Used rarely in some Italian transcriptions.) If numbers appear between other measures, this is number six.

⠶ 1. F as an eighth, a 128th, or as a member of a braille rhythmic group. See grouping, page 178.

2. In margin: measure number seven.

3. In neumatic notation: F as an eighth note; the basic rhythmic unit or pulse.

4. When preceded and followed by a space: F as a double whole note. (Used rarely in some Italian transcriptions.) If numbers appear between other measures, this is number seven.

⠶ ⠦ ⠴ ⠖ In zither music: *Griffbrett* strings; chords and intervals of this part generally read down.

⠲ 1. G as an eighth, a 128th, or as a member of a braille rhythmic group. See grouping, page 178.

2. In margin: measure number eight.

3. In neumatic notation: G as an eighth note; the basic rhythmic unit or pulse.

4. When preceded and followed by a space: G as a double whole note. (Used rarely in some Italian transcriptions.) If numbers appear between other measures, this is number eight.

⠆⠆   1. A as an eighth, a 128th, or as a member of a braille rhythmic group. See grouping, page 178.

2. In margin: measure number nine.

3. In neumatic notation: A as an eighth note; the basic rhythmic unit or pulse.

4. In organ music: roman numeral I to indicate first manual; usually found in parentheses.

Example: ⠆⠆ ⠒⠆ ⠆⠒ ⠆⠆

5. When preceded and followed by a space: A as a double whole note. (Used rarely in some Italian transcriptions.) If numbers appear between other measures, this is number nine.

⠒⠆ ⠒⠆   In organ music: roman numeral II to indicate second manual; usually found in parentheses.

⠒⠆ ⠒⠆ ⠒⠆   In organ music: roman numeral III to indicate third manual; usually found in parentheses.

⠒⠆ ⠆⠒   In organ music: roman numeral IV to indicate fourth manual; usually found in parentheses.

⠒⠆   1. B as an eighth, a 128th, or as a member of a braille rhythmic group. See grouping, page 178.

2. In margin: measure number zero; indicates an incomplete measure at the beginning of a piece or movement.

3. In neumatic notation: B as an eighth note; the basic rhythmic unit or pulse.

⠒⠒

4. When preceded and followed by a space: B as a double whole note. (Used rarely in some Italian transcriptions.)

⠰⠆ 1. Following a whole note or a whole rest: suffix for a double whole note or a double whole rest. See definitions 3, 4, 5, and 9.

2. When preceded and followed by a space: dotted bar line. See definition 8.

3. In keyboard music: fifth finger on the preceding note or interval. If another fingering sign follows, see ⠰⠆ , definition 1, page 1.

4. In organ pedal part: change from toe to heel.

5. In string music: open string or natural harmonic, depending on context; applies to the preceding note. If a fingering precedes this sign, ⠐⠆ is a natural harmonic played by the finger indicated; if a fingering follows, ⠰⠆ indicates open string.

6. In music for Japanese samisen: *surisage* (loosen string with left hand); follows the note.

7. In music for Japanese koto: *hiki-iro* (loosen string with left hand); follows the note.

8. In Spanner short-form scoring: minor chord; immediately follows the note name and rhythmic value. Example: ⠩⠰⠆ is a C minor chord with the duration of a whole note.

9. In chant notation: bar line or dotted bar line if preceded and followed by a space; if it immediately follows a note, it indicates a reciting note.

10   *In braille edition pages 14 and 15*

10. In Rodenberg system of figured bass: indication that the preceding chord has the duration of a half note.

11. In some vertical score and bar-by-bar transcriptions: section sign indicating the beginning or the end of a part-measure in-accord; occurs only in transcriptions where ⠦ is used as an in-accord sign. See ⠦ , definition 9, page 32.

12. In pre-1929 transcriptions: 64th note rhythmic values; the preceding note or chord should be played as a series of reiterated 64th notes. If used twice and there appear to be too many beats in the measure, the notes should be alternated as 64ths. See also ⠦ ⠦ , which is another form of the sign.

13. In neumatic notation: provision for an extra syllable in one or more verses of the text; an extra note of the preceding pitch may be added at this point.

⠦ ⠦   In organ pedal part: toe of either foot on preceding note or interval.

⠦ ⠦   In pre-1929 transcriptions: the preceding note or chord is played as a series of reiterated or alternated 64ths. This form of the sign is used when fingering is present. For an example see ⠦ ⠦ , definition 3, page 2.

⠦ ⠦ ⠦   In Spanner short-form scoring: minor sixth chord; immediately follows the note name and rhythmic value.

⠆⠆ ⠆⠿ ⠿⠿

Example: ⠿⠆ ⠆⠆ ⠆⠿ ⠿⠿ is a C minor sixth chord with the duration of a whole note.

⠆⠆ ⠆⠿ ⠿⠿ In Spanner short-form scoring: minor seventh chord; immediately follows the note name and rhythmic value. Example: ⠿⠆ ⠆⠆ ⠆⠿ ⠿⠿ is a C minor seventh chord with the duration of a whole note.

⠆⠆ ⠿⠿ ⠿⠿ ⠿⠿ ⠆⠆ In Spanner short-form scoring: minor seventh chord with flat fifth; follows the sign indicating the note name and rhythmic value.

⠆⠆ ⠆⠆ In organ pedal part: heel or either foot on preceding note or interval.

⠆⠆ 1. Third finger on the preceding note or interval. See ⠆⠆ , definition 1, page 1.

2. In keyboard music: usually third finger; occasionally unison interval, especially in vertical score format.

3. In organ pedal part: right toe on the preceding note or interval. See ⠆⠆ , definition 2, page 1.

4. In percussion music: right hand for preceding note. A left hand sign following immediately is an alternative.

5. In solo vocal music: three vowels are sung on the preceding note. In braille the corresponding syllables in the text are surrounded by quotation marks.

6. In choral music: unison of two parts on the preceding note. Used primarily in vertical score format, it replaces an

12

interval sign. If more than two parts meet, this unison sign is repeated for each part. The sign is also found in vertical score keyboard music.

7. When preceded and followed by a space: bar line.

8. In Rodenberg system of figured bass: indication that the preceding note or chord has the duration of a 16th note.

9. In pre-1929 transcriptions: 16th note rhythmic values; the preceding note or chord should be played as a series of reiterated 16th notes. If used twice and there appear to be too many beats in the measure, the notes should be alternated as 16ths. See also ⠆⠆ which is another form of the sign.

10. In French transcriptions of neumatic notation: *tristropha;* the preceding note is held for three pulses.

⠆⠆   In pre-1929 transcriptions: the preceding note or chord is played as a series of reiterated or alternated 16th notes. This form of the sign is used when fingering is present. For an example see ⠒⠒ , definition 3, page 2.

⠆⠒   1. In keyboard music: third finger for the preceding note with the second fingering omitted in a passage of alternative fingerings.

2. In string music: third finger followed by a continuation line; the third finger remains on the string until the finger sign is repeated preceded by dot 6.

3. In a keyboard passage for alternating hands and feet: organ pedal notes. It has this meaning only when the

⠍

signs ⠁⠄ and ⠃⠄ are used for alternating hands. See ⠁⠄, definition 4, page 3.

⠍ Whole or 16th rest. If preceded and followed by a space, one measure of rest regardless of time signature; if written two or three times, two or three measures of rest. If there are more than three measures of rest, a number will precede this sign to specify the total. Within a measure this may be either a whole or a 16th rest according to the number of beats remaining. A 16th rest may be the first member of a braille group of 16th notes. See grouping, page 178.

⠍⠙⠄ *Mano destra* (right hand).

⠍⠅ Double whole rest.

⠍⠎⠄ *Mano sinistra* (left hand).

⠍⠄⠙⠄ *Main droit* (right hand).

⠍⠄⠛⠄ *Main gauche* (left hand).

⠍⠘⠍⠍ Double whole rest.

⠝ 1. C as a half or a 32nd note.

2. Half or 32nd note with no specific pitch as in metronome markings or percussion music.

3. In Spanner short-form scoring and in the Canadian melody-chord system: C major chord with the duration of a half note. See ⠒⠰ ⠒⠆, definition 1, page 121.

4. In neumatic notation: C as the first note of a neume. In early French transcriptions, sometimes indicates the note A with a *tenuto* mark.

⠆⠒ ⠒⠆ ⠒⠆ ⠒⠒ ⠒⠆   Metronome marking: half note equals 60. The third element of a metronome marking is a number or a rhythmic value.

⠒⠰   1. D as a half or a 32nd note.

2. In Spanner short-form scoring and in the Canadian melody-chord system: D major chord with the duration of a half note. See ⠒⠰ ⠒⠆ , definition 1, page 121.

3. In neumatic notation: D as the first note of a neume. In early French transcriptions, sometimes indicates the note D with a *tenuto* mark.

⠒⠂   1. E as a half or a 32nd note.

2. In Spanner short-form scoring and in the Canadian melody-chord system: E major chord with the duration of a half note. See ⠒⠂ ⠒⠆ , definition 1, page 121.

3. In neumatic notation: E as the first note of a neume. In early French transcriptions, sometimes indicates the note E with a *tenuto* mark.

⠒⠆ ⠒⠆ ⠒⠆ ⠒⠆   Abbreviation for *pédale* (pedal) part.

⠿ 1. F as a half or a 32nd note.

2. In Spanner short-form scoring and in the Canadian melody-chord system: F major chord with the duration of a half note. See ⠆⠒ , definition 1, page 121.

3. In neumatic notation: F as the first note of a neume. In early French transcriptions, sometimes indicates the note F with a *tenuto* mark.

⠶ 1. G as a half or a 32nd note.

2. In Spanner short-form scoring and in the Canadian melody-chord system: G major chord with the duration of a half note. See ⠒⠶ , definition 1, page 121.

3. In neumatic notation: G as the first note of a neume. In early French transcriptions, sometimes indicates the note G with a *tenuto* mark.

⠆ 1. A as a half or a 32nd note.

2. In Spanner short-form scoring and in the Canadian melody-chord system: A major chord with the duration of a half note. See ⠒⠶ , definition 1, page 121.

3. In neumatic notation: A as the first note of a neume. In early French transcriptions, sometimes indicates the note A with a *tenuto* mark.

⠆⠶ 1. A as a dotted half or a dotted 32nd note.

2. In choral music: abbreviation for soprano.

16

⠿ 1. B as a half or a 32nd note.

2. In Spanner short-form scoring and in the Canadian melody-chord system: B major chord with the duration of a half note. See ⠿ ⠿ , definition 1, page 121.

3. When surrounded by parentheses: abbreviation for turn, referring to a page turn in the print music.

4. In neumatic notation: B as the first note of a neume. In early French transcriptions, sometimes indicates the note B with a *tenuto* mark.

⠿ ⠿ 1. B as a dotted half or a dotted 32nd note.

2. In choral music: abbreviation for tenor.

⠿ ⠿ ⠿ ⠿ Abbreviation for Transcriber's Note.

⠿ Half or 32nd rest; 32nd rest may be the first member of a braille group of 32nds. See grouping, page 178.

⠿ 1. Quarter or 64th rest; 64th rest may be the first member of a braille group of 64ths. See grouping, page 178.

2. In organ music: roman numeral V to indicate fifth manual; usually found in parentheses.

⠿ 1. Eighth or 128th rest; 128th rest may be the first member of a braille group of 128ths. See grouping, page 178.

2. When preceded and followed by a space: double whole rest. (Used rarely in some Italian transcriptions.)

⠿ 1. C as a whole or a 16th note.

⠓⠓ ⠓⠓

2. Whole or 16th note with no specific pitch, as in metronome markings or percussion music.

3. In Spanner short-form scoring and in the Canadian melody-chord system: C major chord with the duration of a whole note. See ⠓⠓ ⠓⠓ , definition 1, page 121.

4. In neumatic notation: C as a *quilisma*.

⠓⠓ ⠓⠓ C as a double whole note or as a reciting note.

⠓⠓ ⠓⠓ ⠓⠓ ⠓⠓ ⠓⠓ Metronome marking: whole note equals 54. The third element of a metronome marking is a number or a rhythmic value.

⠓⠓ ⠓⠓ ⠓⠓ ⠓⠓ C as a double whole note.

⠓⠓ 1. D as a whole or a 16th note.

2. In Spanner short-form scoring and in the Canadian melody-chord system: D major chord with the duration of a whole note. See ⠓⠓ ⠓⠓ , definition 1, page 121.

3. In neumatic notation: D as a *quilisma*.

⠓⠓ ⠓⠓ D as a double whole note or as a reciting note.

⠓⠓ ⠓⠓ ⠓⠓ ⠓⠓ D as a double whole note.

⠓⠓ 1. E as a whole or a 16th note.

2. In Spanner short-form scoring and in the Canadian

In braille edition pages 24 and 25

melody-chord system: E major chord with the duration of a whole note. See ⠲⠆ ⠢⠆ , definition 1, page 121.

3. In neumatic notation: E as a *quilisma*.

⠩⠆ ⠶⠆   E as a double whole note or as a reciting note.

⠩⠆ ⠶⠆ ⠩⠆ ⠶⠆   E as a double whole note.

⠿   1. Full cell; used in this dictionary to clarify the position of dots; not a part of any two or three cell music sign except the next two signs.

2. F as a whole or a 16th note.

3. In Spanner short-form scoring and in the Canadian melody-chord system: F major chord with the duration of a whole note. See ⠲⠆ ⠶⠆ , definition 1, page 121.

4. In chant notation: words surrounded by this sign are sung on the reciting note.

5. In neumatic notation: F as a *quilisma*.

⠿⠆ ⠶⠆   F as a double whole note or as a reciting note.

⠿⠆ ⠶⠆ ⠿⠆ ⠶⠆   F as a double whole note.

⠯   1. G as a whole or a 16th note.

2. In Spanner short-form scoring and in the Canadian melody-chord system: G major chord with the duration of a whole note. See ⠲⠆ ⠯⠆ , definition 1, page 121.

3. In neumatic notation: G as a *quilisma*.

⠶⠶ G as a double whole note or as a reciting note.

⠶⠦⠶⠶ G as a double whole note.

⠦ 1. A as a whole or a 16th note.

2. In Spanner short-form scoring and in the Canadian melody-chord system: A major chord with the duration of a whole note. See ⠦⠴ , definition 1, page 121.

3. In neumatic notation: A as a *quilisma.*

⠦⠴ A as a double whole note or as a reciting note.

⠦⠦⠦⠦ A as a double whole note.

⠴ 1. B as a whole or a 16th note.

2. In Spanner short-form scoring and in the Canadian melody-chord system: B major chord with the duration of a whole note. See ⠦⠴ , definition 1, page 121.

3. In neumatic notation: B as a *quilisma.*

⠴⠦ B as a double whole note or as a reciting note.

⠴⠦⠴⠴ B as a double whole note.

⠡ 1. Natural; modifies the sign that follows. In a key signature the natural indicates cancellation of a previous sharp or flat. A natural that precedes an ornament sign

20

applies to the upper auxiliary note of the ornament unless preceded by dot 6; in that case, it applies to the lower auxiliary note of the ornament.

2. When followed by a space, double bar, or music hyphen: marks the end of a passage to be repeated because of a *segno* or a *da capo*.

3. In the text of liturgical music: the vowel A with tonic stress. Example: ⠦ ⠒⠆ ⠰⠦ ⠒⠒ ⠦⠦ ⠒⠰ ⠦⠒

⠒⠒ ⠒⠒   In string music: obsolete form of thumb sign.

⠒⠆ ⠰⠰   Release sustaining pedal; follows the last note of the sustained passage.

⠰⠰ ⠒⠒   1. In string music: thumb. Since placement of this sign varies, it is necessary to examine the score to determine whether this sign affects the following note or the preceding note. See definition 2.

2. In guitar music: the following note is plucked with the thumb of the right hand. The print indication usually is *p*.

⠰⠰ ⠒⠒ ⠒⠒   In string music: thumb on the first string.

⠰⠰ ⠒⠒ ⠒⠆   In string music: thumb on the second string.

⠰⠰ ⠰⠰ ⠒⠆   In string music: thumb on the third string.

⠰⠆ ⠒⠆ ⠒⠆   In string music: thumb on the fourth string.

⠠⠠ In string music: artificial harmonic; the next note or interval is a diamond-shaped note in print.

⠠⠠ In music for Japanese instruments: the melody of another instrument begins with this sign and ends with ⠠⠠

⠠⠠ In music for Japanese instruments: end of inserted passage.

⠠⠠⠠ In keyboard music: release and depress pedal as the following note is sounded or during the following rest.

⠠⠠ In string music: end of a continuation line for fingering. See ⠠⠠ , definition 2.

⠠⠠ 1. In unmeasured music or *cadenza:* beginning of a group of notes that will be repeated.

   2. In string music: line of continuation for the fingering of the following note. The end of this line is marked ⠠⠠ There may be more than one line, each applying to a different finger.

⠠⠠ *Crescendo* and *diminuendo* (diverging and converging lines) on the single note or chord that follows.

⠠ 1. Flat; modifies the sign that follows. A flat that precedes an ornament sign applies to the upper auxiliary

22

In braille edition pages 29 and 30

note of the ornament unless preceded by dot 6; in that case, it applies to the lower auxiliary note of the ornament.

2. In a heading: key signature of one flat; may be preceded by a number to indicate key signatures of more than three flats.

3. When preceded and followed by a space: change to the key signature of one flat.

4. In the text of liturgical music: the vowel E with tonic stress. Example: ⠶ ⠦ ⠶ ⠮ ⠦ ⠦ ⠶ ⠦

⠦ ⠶   In guitar music: end of a continuation line following a fret sign.

⠦ ⠶ ⠶ ⠶ ⠶   Ornament; *Bebung*. In print a curve over dots placed above a note. The number of dots in the print regulates the number of dot-1 characters in the braille sign. See also ⠂ ⠦ ⠦ ⠦ ⠦ , page 85.

⠦ ⠒   1. For bowed instruments: down bow; if written twice in succession, the sign is doubled.

2. For plucked instruments: down stroke; if written twice in succession, the sign is doubled. See definition 3.

3. For harp: downward direction when used before an *arpeggio* or *glissando* sign.

4. For keyboard or wind instruments: downward direction when used before a *glissando* or slur sign.

5. For accordion: draw the bellows.

⠶⠶ 1. In keyboard music: depress sustaining pedal.

2. In instrumental music; slight dip in pitch (small inverted arch in print); applies to next note.

3. In music for plucked instruments: full *barré* on the following chord. If fingering is indicated, the finger sign follows the last interval sign of the chord.

4. In accordion music: either draw or push to change the direction of the bellows.

⠶⠶ 1. Double bar; usually the final double bar of a piece or movement.

2. In chant notation: end of phrase or melody.

⠶⠶⠶ 1. Double bar; usually the end of a section rather than the end of a piece or movement.

2. In chant notation: pause or breath mark.

⠶⠶ 1. Pause, *fermata,* or hold on the preceding note or rest.

2. In neumatic notation: bar line if preceded and followed by a space; if not preceded by a space, horizontal line above the preceding note to indicate a slight retardation.

3. In chant notation: light double bar indicating a pause in the music.

⠶⠶ 1. Double flat; modifies the sign that follows.

2. In a heading: key signature of two flats.

24   *In braille edition pages 31-33*

⠣⠂⠄

3. When preceded and followed by a space: change to the key signature of two flats.

⠣⠣⠣ 1. In a heading: key signature of three flats.

2. When preceded and followed by a space: change to the key signature of three flats.

⠣⠂ 1. Braille music comma; indicates an unusual pattern of notes across a bar line or across beats. The sign surrounds the group or groups that are unusual. In complex situations the final comma is followed by dot 3. See definition 2.

2. Rhythmic value separator; when one measure contains notes of differing rhythmic values that could be read the same (such as half notes and 32nds), this sign is found between the different values. In the following example, the first note is a half note, and the next four are 32nds.

Example: ⠼⠙⠲ ⠐⠝⠣⠂⠝⠝⠝⠝⠋⠹

See definition 3.

3. Coincidence of beats; precedes notes that occur simultaneously in both hands during complex music, a *cadenza*, or an unmeasured passage. See also ⠰⠆, definition 2, page 109.

⠣⠂⠄ Final braille music comma; used only in complex situations to indicate resumption of a normal pattern of notes.

⠰⠆ ⠰⠂

⠰⠆ ⠰⠆   1. Print repeat sign; double bar preceded by dots; repeat preceding section of music. See   ⠰⠆ ⠰⠂   below.

  2. In some Italian press braille music: repeat the following section of music. In this case, the sign is preceded by a space.

⠰⠆ ⠰⠂   Print repeat sign; double bar followed by dots; repeat following section of music. See   ⠰⠆ ⠰⠆   above.

⠰⠆ ⠒⠆   Full-measure in-accord; connects sections of music, usually contrapuntal voices or parts. In print these sections are written vertically rather than horizontally. Each section of music so connected contains a whole measure of rhythmic value. See in-accords, page 169.

⠨⠆ ⠒⠆   1. For bowed instruments: up bow; if written twice in succession, the sign is doubled.

  2. For plucked instruments: up stroke; if written twice in succession, the sign is doubled.

  3. For harp: upward direction when used before an *arpeggio* or *glissando* sign.

  4. For keyboard or wind instruments: upward direction when used before a *glissando* or slur sign.

  5. For accordion: push the bellows.

  6. In Rodenberg system of figured bass: flat sign standing alone.

⠨⠆ ⠒⠆ ⠒⠒   Slur with an upward direction preceding a note.

⠨⠆ ⠒⠆ ⠒⠆ ⠒⠆   Upward *glissando* into the following note.

26   *In braille edition pages 34 and 35*

⠼⠂ 1. Sharp; modifies the sign that follows. A sharp that precedes an ornament sign applies to the upper auxiliary note of the ornament unless preceded by dot 6; in that case, it applies to the lower auxiliary note of the ornament.

2. In a heading: key signature of one sharp; may be preceded by a number to indicate key signatures of more than three sharps.

3. When preceded and followed by a space: change to the key signature of one sharp.

4. In the text of liturgical music: the vowel *i* with tonic stress.

Example: ⠼⠼ ⠼⠼ ⠼⠼ ⠼⠼ ⠼⠼ ⠼⠼ ⠼⠼ ⠼⠼ ⠼⠼ ⠼⠼

5. When immediately preceded by an octave sign: the passage that follows is written in a method known as substitution. See ⠼⠼ ⠼⠼ ⠼⠼ , page 93.

⠼⠼ ⠼⠼ In string music: the following note should be played on the first string. This sign is doubled either if it appears twice in succession or if only the second half of the sign (dot 1) is repeated.

⠼⠼ ⠼⠼ In string music: the following note should be played on the second string. This sign is doubled either if it appears twice in succession or if only the second half of the sign (dots 1-2) is repeated.

⠶⠂ 1. In string music: the following note should be played on the fifth string. This sign is doubled either if it appears twice in succession or if only the second half of the sign (dots 1-3) is repeated.

2. In pre-1929 transcriptions: open string.

⠶⠆ In string music: the following note should be played on the third string. This sign is doubled either if it appears twice in succession or if only the second half of the sign (dots 1-2-3) is repeated.

⠩⠩ 1. Double sharp; modifies the sign that follows.

2. In a heading: key signature of two sharps.

3. When preceded and followed by a space: change to the key signature of two sharps.

⠩⠩⠩ 1. In a heading: key signature of three sharps.

2. When preceded and followed by a space: change to the key signature of three sharps.

⠆⠒ In string music: the following note should be played on the fourth string. This sign is doubled either if it appears twice in succession or if only the second half of the sign (dot 4) is repeated.

⠆⠂ In string music: the following note should be played on the sixth string. This sign is doubled either if it appears twice

In braille edition pages 37 and 38

in succession or if only the second half of the sign (dots 2-3) is repeated.

⠲⠆ ⠆⠲   In string music: stay in the same position.

⠲⠒ ⠒⠲   1. In string music: seventh string.

   2. In Rodenberg system of figured bass: sharp standing alone.

⠲⠒⠲   In music for koto: eighth string.

⠆⠒⠲   In music for koto: ninth string.

⠲⠒⠒   In music for koto: twelfth string.

⠲⠒⠒   In music for koto: tenth string.

⠲⠒⠲   In music for koto: eleventh string.

⠲⠒⠆   In music for koto: thirteenth string.

⠹   1. C as a quarter or a 64th note.

   2. Quarter or 64th note with no specific pitch as in metronome markings or percussion music.

   3. In Spanner short-form scoring and in the Canadian melody-chord system: C major chord with the duration of a quarter note. See ⠹⠯ , definition 1, page 121.

⠆⠆ ⠆⠆ ⠆⠆ ⠆⠆ ⠆⠆

4. In the text of liturgical music: the vowel *o* with tonic stress. Example: ⠆⠆ ⠆⠆ ⠆⠆ ⠆⠆ ⠆⠆ ⠆⠆

5. In neumatic notation: liquescent note C.

⠆⠆ ⠆⠆ ⠆⠆ ⠆⠆ ⠆⠆ Metronome marking: quarter note equals 72. The third element of a metronome marking is a number or a rhythmic value.

⠆⠆ 1. D as a quarter or a 64th note.

2. In Spanner short-form scoring and in the Canadian melody-chord system: D major chord with the duration of a quarter note. See ⠆⠆ ⠆⠆ , definition 1, page 121.

3. In the text of liturgical music: the vowel *u* with tonic stress.

4. In neumatic notation: liquescent note D.

⠆⠆ 1. E as a quarter or a 64th note.

2. In Spanner short-form scoring and in the Canadian melody-chord system: E major chord with the duration of a quarter note. See ⠆⠆ ⠆⠆ , definition 1, page 121.

3. In neumatic notation: liquescent note E.

⠆⠆ 1. F as a quarter or a 64th note.

2. In Spanner short-form scoring and in the Canadian melody-chord system: F major chord with the duration of a quarter note. See ⠆⠆ ⠆⠆ , definition 1, page 121.

3. In neumatic notation: liquescent note F.

In braille edition pages 39 and 40

⠦ 1. G as a quarter or a 64th note.

2. In Spanner short-form scoring and in the Canadian melody-chord system: G major chord with the duration of a quarter note. See ⠔⠦ , definition 1, page 121.

3. In neumatic notation: liquescent note G.

⠴ 1. A as a quarter or a 64th note.

2. In Spanner short-form scoring and in the Canadian melody-chord system: A major chord with the duration of a quarter note. See ⠔⠴ , definition 1, page 121.

3. In neumatic notation: liquescent note A.

⠒ 1. B as a quarter or a 64th note.

2. In Spanner short-form scoring and in the Canadian melody-chord system: B major chord with the duration of a quarter note. See ⠔⠒ , definition 1, page 121.

3. In neumatic notation: liquescent note B.

⠂ 1. Fourth finger on the preceding note or interval. See ⠂ , definition 1, page 1.

2. In organ pedal part: right heel on the preceding note or interval. See ⠂ , definition 2, page 1.

3. The number one in lower-cell position. After a hand sign or marginal abbreviation, the first part; i.e., first violin, first piano, or first clarinet. If preceded by a number sign, see ⠼⠂ , page 54.

4. In ukulele chord notation: first fret.

⠢⠂

5. In music for Japanese koto: *ato-oshi* (press the string with the left hand); follows the note.

6. In music for Japanese samisen: *suriage* (press the string with the left hand); follows the note.

7. In vocal music; half breath.

8. In Rodenberg figured bass system: print dash or continuation line.

9. In some vertical score and bar-by-bar formats: in-accord sign; indicates a whole-measure in-accord unless ⠢⠂ appears in the measure to separate the part of the measure that contains the in-accord from the remainder of the measure. In that case it becomes a part-measure in-accord. The first line of the example below contains whole-measure in-accords; the second line contains a part-measure in-accord.

Example:

10. In pre-1929 transcriptions: fourth finger if other fingering is present. Otherwise, 32nd note rhythmic values; the preceding note or chord should be played as a series of reiterated 32nd notes. If used twice and there appear to be too many beats in the measure, the notes should be alternated as 32nds. See ⠢⠂ ⠢⠂ , page 33.

11. In French neumatic notation: *quadistropha;* the preceding note should be held for four pulses.

In braille edition pages 42 and 43

⠰⠆ 1. In music for Japanese koto: *tsuki-iro* (with left hand press down and then immediately let the string free); follows the note.

2. In music for Japanese samisen: *suriage* and *surisage* (with the left hand press down and then immediately let the string free); follows the note.

⠆⠒⠰ In music for Japanese koto or samisen: *yuri* (with the left hand alternately press down and free the string a few times at the left side of the bridge); follows the note.

⠰⠆ In pre-1929 transcriptions: 32nd note rhythmic values. This form of the sign is used when the music contains fingering; the preceding note or chord should be played as a series of reiterated 32nd notes. If used twice and there appear to be too many beats in the measure, the notes should be alternated as 32nds. For an example see ⠒⠆ , definition 3, page 2.

⠰⠆ After marginal part or hand sign: first and second parts. Example: ⠨⠜⠆⠆⠆ indicates the part for first and second clarinet.

⠆⠰ In string music: fourth finger followed by a continuation line; the fourth finger remains on the string until the finger sign is repeated preceded by dot 6.

⠆⠆ 1. Triplet; precedes the notes. If written twice in succession, the sign is doubled.

2. After a hand sign or marginal abbreviation: second part, i.e., second violin or second clarinet.

3. In ukulele chord notation: second fret.

4. In harmonic analysis: arabic numeral two; always follows a roman numeral immediately; not preceded by a numeral sign.

5. In neumatic notation: *pressus*; two notes of the same pitch are sung as one long note equal to two pulses. This sign (dots 2-3) replaces the second of the two notes.

⠒ 1. Interval of a seventh; see intervals and chords, page 172. If written twice in succession, the sign is doubled.

2. In ukulele chord notation: third fret.

3. In the Canadian melody-chord system: seventh chord; follows the sign for the note name and rhythmic value. Example: ⠆⠒ is a C seventh chord with the duration of a whole note.

4. In harmonic analysis: arabic numeral three; always follows a roman numeral immediately; not preceded by a numeral sign.

5. In Spanner system of figured bass: number three.

6. In Rodenberg system of figured bass: number seven.

7. In the note-for-note method 2 only: trill sign.

⠢⠆ When preceded by a space: change of print staff.

34 *In braille edition pages 44-46*

⠆⠆ ⠒⠒ In organ pedal part: cross the foot behind; precedes the note to be played by the foot that crosses behind.

⠆⠆ ⠢⠢ 1. In text of chant notation: the preceding syllable continues after the reciting note and is also sung on the next note of music; a print dash.

2. In vocal music with two languages: prefix indicating the text in the second language.

⠢⠢ 1. Ornament; turn between two notes. The sign generally precedes the principal note of the turn; fingering, if given, follows the note. Occasionally the sign is written after the note (as in print); in that case the fingering still follows the principal note.

2. In ukulele chord notation: fourth fret.

3. In Canadian melody-chord system: diminished chord; follows the note name and rhythmic value. Example: ⠦⠦ ⠢⠢ is a C diminished chord with the duration of a whole note.

4. In harmonic analysis: arabic numeral four; always follows a roman numeral immediately; not preceded by a numeral sign.

5. In Spanner system of figured bass: number four except when preceded by a hyphen (dots 3-6) in the horizontal arrangement of signs. In this case it is a turn. See page 157.

6. In music for Japanese instruments: alternate symbol for plectrum upstroke. See also ⠢⠢ ⠒⠒ , definition 2, page 26.

⠆⠆ ⠒⠆

7. In the note-for-note method only: C as a member of a chord.

⠆⠆ ⠒⠆   Ornament; inverted turn beginning on the following note or interval. Fingering, if given, will follow that note or interval.

⠆⠆ ⠒⠆ ⠰⠆   Ornament; trill beginning with an inverted turn.

⠆⠆ ⠒⠆ ⠰⠆ ⠒⠆   Ornament; long (extended) inverted (upper) mordent beginning with an inverted turn.

⠆⠆ ⠒⠆ ⠰⠆ ⠆⠆ ⠒⠆   Ornament; long (extended) mordent (lower mordent) beginning with an inverted turn.

⠆⠆ ⠒⠆ ⠰⠆ ⠆⠆ ⠰⠰   Ornament; trill beginning with an inverted turn and ending with a normal turn.

⠆⠆ ⠒⠆   1. Ornament; trill beginning with a turn.
2. In some Italian transcriptions: series of short *crescendos* (diverging lines). The final *crescendo* is written with the sign ⠒⠒ ⠒⠆ unless a new dynamic indication eliminates the need for an ending sign.

⠆⠆ ⠰⠆ ⠒⠆   Ornament; trill ending with an upward curve in the print.

36

⠒⠂⠢ ⠒⠂⠢ ⠒⠂⠒ Ornament; trill ending with a downward curve in the print.

⠒⠂⠢ ⠒⠂⠢ ⠒⠂⠒ Ornament; long (extended) inverted (upper) mordent beginning with a turn.

⠒⠂⠢ ⠒⠂⠢ ⠒⠂⠢ ⠒⠂⠒ Ornament; long (extended) mordent (lower mordent) beginning with a turn.

⠒⠂⠢ ⠒⠂⠢ ⠒⠂⠢ ⠒⠂⠢ Ornament; trill beginning and ending with a turn.

⠢ 1. Ornament; grace note. Affects the following note and any of its intervals. If written twice in succession, the sign is doubled.

2. Preceding a fingering, an accidental, or a word abbreviation: parentheses; used once to represent both the opening and closing parentheses that surround the individual sign in print.

3. In percussion music: flam.

4. In ukulele chord notation: fifth fret.

5. In Canadian melody-chord system: augmented chord; follows the note name and rhythmic value. Example: ⠶⠢ is a C augmented chord with the duration of a whole note.

6. In English chord-symbol system: the abbreviation *sus*. Example: ⠢ ⠢ ⠢ ⠢ ⠢ ⠢ is a B flat sus4 chord.

⠢⠉

7. In harmonic analysis: arabic numeral five; always follows a roman numeral immediately; not preceded by a numeral sign.

8. In Spanner system of figured bass: number five except when preceded by a hyphen (dots 3-6) in the horizontal arrangement of signs. In this case it is a grace note. See page 157.

9. In Rodenberg system of figured bass: used between two interval signs to mean that those numbers appear in print side by side rather than in a vertical column.

10. Variant sign; precedes and follows a passage that is an alternate version of a previous passage. When there are several variants, each is preceded by a number. A number following indicates the number of measures in the passage. For example, if two variations are shown and each of them contains three measures, the variants are preceded consecutively by the following signs:

⠼⠁⠢⠼⠉ ⠼⠃⠢⠼⠉

11. In chant notation: prefix to indicate a liquescent note.

12. In the note-for-note method only: D as a member of a chord.

⠢⠉ In music for plucked instruments: partial *barré* affecting the intervals that follow.

⠢⠉⠃ In music for plucked instruments: partial *barré* affecting the next two notes.

:: :: :: In music for plucked instruments: partial *barré* affecting the next three notes.

:: ::   1. In the text of chant music: print cross.
  2. Doubled form of the grace note sign.

:: :: Obsolete form of music asterisk.

:: :: :: Variant or alternate presentation of two bars of music. See :: , definition 10.

:: :: Parentheses around a dynamic marking or word abbreviation; used once to represent both the opening and closing parentheses that surround the individual abbreviation or sign in print.

:: :: :: Ornament; *acciaccatura* (grace note within a chord); placed before the member of a chord that is played as a short grace note. This member may be the named note or an interval of the chord.

::   1. Ornament; trill on the note or interval that follows. If preceded by a sharp, flat, or natural sign, the accidental applies to the upper note of the trill. If fingering is given for the trill, it follows the note name or interval sign.
  2. In ukulele chord notation: sixth fret.

⠒⠒ ⠒⠒

3. Preceding an organ stop: plus sign indicating the addition of the stop.

4. In Canadian melody-chord system: major seventh chord; follows the sign for the note name and rhythmic value. Example: ⠒⠒ ⠒⠒ is a C major seventh chord with the duration of a whole note.

5. In harmonic analysis: arabic numeral six; always follows a roman numeral immediately; not preceded by a numeral sign.

6. In Spanner system of figured bass: number six except when preceded by a hyphen (dots 3-6) in the horizontal arrangement of signs. In this case it is a trill. See page 157.

7. In the note-for-note method: E as a member of a chord.

⠒⠒ ⠒⠒ 1. Ornament; trill ending with a turn.

2. In some Italian transcriptions: series of short *decrescendos* (converging lines). The final *decrescendo* is written as ⠒⠒ ⠒⠒ unless a new dynamic indication eliminates the need for an ending sign.

⠒⠒ ⠒⠒ ⠒⠒ Ornament; trill ending with an inverted turn.

⠒⠒ 1. When preceded and followed by a space: braille repeat; repeat the preceding measure. If there is a tie at the end of that measure it should not be included in the repeat unless this sign is followed by a tie sign.

2. When preceded by a space and followed by a number: braille repeat; repeat the preceding measure that number of

times. Example: ⠶ ⠶ ⠶ . Repeat preceding measure three times.

3. When preceded by a space: opening literary parenthesis; a whole word or a group of words is surrounded by parentheses and separated from the music by spacing or by placement on a separate line.

4. Preceding or following an in-accord sign: braille repeat; repeat the corresponding part of the preceding measure. If this repeat sign is the only music character before an in-accord sign, repeat the section that was before the in-accord sign in the preceding measure; if this sign is the only music character following the in-accord sign, repeat the music following the in-accord sign of the previous measure. If the repeat sign appears within a measure of music at some other point, see definition 5.

5. Within a measure: braille repeat; repeat part of that measure. The length of the repeat is determined by counting the beats before and after the repeat and comparing that count to the time signature. The repeat does not include a tie on the last note or chord of the passage to be repeated.

6. When preceded by an octave sign: braille repeat; the repeated passage is in a new octave. The first note of the repeat is in the octave indicated.

7. In a heading: equal sign for a metronome marking.

8. In ukulele chord notation: seventh fret.

9. In harmonic analysis: arabic numeral seven; always follows a roman numeral immediately; not preceded by a numeral sign.

⠿⠿ 10. In the Spanner system of figured bass: number seven except when preceded by a hyphen (dots 3-6) in the horizontal arrangement of signs. In this case it is a repeat sign. See page 157.

11. In the note-for-note method only: G as a member of a chord.

⠿⠿ 1. Rehearsal letter A; usually found in the margin or in a heading. Subsequent letters are also surrounded by parentheses and located similarly. A letter within a paragraph of music may be a rehearsal letter or the indication of a footnote. See definition 2.

2. Footnote A. In some transcriptions footnotes are lettered A, B, etc. The letter is found within parentheses in the music and at the beginning of the explanatory material that is located at the bottom of the same braille page or in a section of footnotes.

⠿⠿ In organ music: first manual.

⠿⠿ In organ music: second manual. Other manuals are similarly indicated by roman numerals placed in parentheses.

⠿⠿ In music for Japanese koto or samisen: *otoshi;* plectrum indication that precedes note.

In braille edition pages 55 and 56

⠒⠒ ⠒⠒ ⠒⠒ Print page turn; appears at the point where the print page should actually be turned.

⠒⠒ ⠒⠒ Repeat three times. In some transcriptions a lower-cell number follows a repeat sign to indicate the number of times the preceding measure should be repeated.

⠒⠒ ⠒⠒ Repeat four times. See definition above.

⠒⠒ ⠒⠒ 1. Within a measure: two part-measure repeats of equal value.

2. In music for the harmonium or organ: the following registration applies to both hands.

⠒⠒ ⠒⠒ ⠒⠒ Part-measure repeats of unequal duration within one measure, with the second repeat of longer duration than the first.

Example: ⠒⠒ ⠒⠒ ⠒⠒   ⠒⠒⠒⠒⠒⠒⠒⠒⠒⠒⠒⠒⠒⠒⠒⠒

In the example, the first beat of four-four time contains four sixteenth notes; the second beat is a repeat of the first. Dot 3 indicates that the second repeat is longer than the first so it includes the first two beats, making four identical groups of sixteenth notes in the measure.

⠒⠒ 1. Staccato; affects the following note or chord. If written twice in succession, the sign is doubled.

2. In Canadian melody-chord system: minor chord; follows the note name and rhythmic value. Example:

⠦⠴

⠽⠦ is a C minor chord with the duration of a whole note.

3. In harmonic analysis: arabic numeral eight; always follows a roman numeral immediately; not preceded by a number sign.

4. In Spanner system of figured bass: number eight except when preceded by a hyphen (dots 3-6) in the horizontal arrangement of signs. In this case it is a staccato sign. See page 157.

5. In the note-for-note method only: G as a member of a chord.

⠦⠴ 1. In the text of vocal music: two or more syllables with vowels sung on the same note. For chant music, see definition 2.

2. In chant notation: each syllable surrounded by quotation marks is sung on two notes. This meaning applies only when hyphens (dots 3-6) appear in the music line, indicating the older method of braille notation. If there are no hyphens or if the slur sign (dots 1-4) is present in the music line, see definition 1.

⠦⠁ In music for plucked instruments: right hand index finger; precedes the note. For combined fingering, see ⠦⠅ .

⠦⠃ In music for plucked instruments: right hand middle finger; precedes the note. For combined fingering, see ⠦⠅ .

⠒⠒ In music for plucked instruments: right hand thumb. Fingering may be combined as in the following example, which should be read up.

Example: ⠲⠒ ⠲⠂ ⠒⠂ ⠒⠆ ⠒⠒ ⠆⠒ ⠆⠆ ⠂⠒ ⠂⠆ ⠂⠂ ⠒⠂

In the example, third octave E is plucked with the thumb, fourth octave G is plucked with the index finger, B is plucked with the middle finger, and fifth octave E is plucked with the ring finger. If the sign ⠂⠂ (dot 3) appears in a combined fingering, the print did not show a fingering for that member of the chord.

⠒⠒ In music for plucked instruments: right hand ring finger; precedes the note.

⠒ 1. Interval of a fifth. See intervals and chords, page 172. If written twice in succession, the sign is doubled.

2. In the text of vocal music: braille repeat sign; the word(s) between this sign and the next ⠒⠂ sign are to be repeated. If this sign is doubled initially, it indicates two repetitions (sing three times). A number preceding the first repetition indicates the number of repetitions to be sung.

3. Preceding organ stop: a minus sign indicating the suppression of a stop.

4. In harmonic analysis: arabic numeral nine; always follows a roman numeral immediately; not preceded by a numeral sign.

5. In Spanner system of figured bass: number nine.

6. In Rodenberg system of figured bass: number five.

⠆⠆ ⠆⠆

7. In the note-for-note method only: A as a member of a chord.

⠆⠆ ⠆⠆ In Anglican chant: pointing symbol within the word line.

⠆⠆ ⠆⠆ Literary asterisk; in chant notation it indicates a change between choirs or chanters.

⠆⠆ 1. Interval of a sixth; see intervals and chords, page 172. If written twice in succession, the sign is doubled.

2. In Canadian melody-chord system: sixth chord; follows the note name and rhythmic value. Example: ⠆⠆ ⠆⠆ is a C sixth chord with the duration of a whole note.

3. In Spanner system of figured bass: number zero.

4. In Rodenberg system of figured bass: number six.

5. When preceded by a space: parallel motion; this part moves parallel to another part at the interval of a sixth (rare). See ⠆⠆ , definition 7, page 172.

6. In the note-for-note method only: B as a member of a chord.

⠆⠆ 1. Interval of a second; see intervals and chords, page 172. If written twice in succession, the sign is doubled.

2. In vocal music: at the beginning of a measure, a warning that the lines will divide into two in-accord parts.

3. In music for plucked instruments: strumming sign placed directly below the note to which it applies. As part of a

46

literary chord symbol, it represents an oblique line; the note following this line should be played in the bass.

4. In Canadian melody-chord system: ninth chord; follows the sign for the note name and rhythmic value. Example: ⠦⠴ is a C ninth chord with the duration of a whole note.

5. In Spanner system of figured bass: oblique stroke standing alone.

6. In Rodenberg system of figured bass: number nine.

7. In registration for accordion music: *tremolo*; may be preceded by ⠒ to indicate augmented *tremolo* or by ⠲ to indicate diminished *tremolo*.

8. In chant notation: short breath mark; quick breath may be taken with no delay of the rhythm. This sign may be found in the word line, melody line, or both.

9. In the note-for-note method 2 only: short grace note.

⠢ 1. Interval of a third; see intervals and chords, page 172. If written twice in succession, the sign is doubled.

2. When preceded and followed by a space: *segno* or sign; the section of music following this sign and ending with the sign ⠶ will be repeated.

3. In literary chord symbols: plus sign.

4. In Spanner system of figured bass: plus sign.

5. In Rodenberg system of figured bass: number three.

6. In chant notation: breath mark indicating that a breath should be taken without a pause in the rhythm. This sign may be found in the word line, melody line, or both.

⠬⠁

7. When preceded by a space: parallel motion; this part moves parallel to another part of the interval of a third (rare). See ⠤ , definition 7, page 80.

8. In the note-for-note method 2 only: whole or part measure repeat, replacing the sign ⠶ .

⠬⠁ When preceded and followed by a space: *segno* A; the section of music following this sign and ending with ⠡ will be repeated. The second half of the sign is the letter A; subsequent *segnos* are indicated by B, C, etc.

⠬⠇ When preceded and followed by a space: *coda* sign (encircled cross in print).

⠼ 1. Interval of a fourth; see intervals and chords, page 172. If written twice in succession, the sign is doubled.

2. If preceded by a space: number sign; the number following this sign may be in upper- or lower-cell position. The next several entries are examples of numbers in both positions.

3. In Rodenberg system of figured bass: number four.

4. In chant notation: full breath mark indicating the end of a phrase; usually indicates a pause in the music. This sign may be found in the word line, melody line, or both.

5. In the note-for-note method 2 only: initial sign for an unusual number of notes on a beat, replacing the sign ⠸ . See ⠸⠆⠄ , page 94.

⠼⠁ 1.   At the margin: measure, staff, or rehearsal number one.

2. In Spanner system of figured bass: dash or horizontal continuation line. In braille this sign may be found after either a number sign or other figuration such as a number or accidental.

3. First ending sign; in popular or dance music with the same tune repeated before and after a middle section, this sign is sometimes used in place of the usual first ending sign ⠰⠂ to distinguish between two sets of first and second endings. If used as a first ending sign, it is not followed by a space.

⠼⠁⠁ 1. At the margin: measure, staff, or rehearsal number eleven.

2. In a heading: section eleven.

3. When preceded and followed by a space: braille repeat; repeat the last eleven measures.

4. In Spanner short-form scoring: eleventh chord; follows the note name and rhythmic value.

5. In Spanner system of figured bass: two continuation lines.

⠼⠁⠁⠁ In Spanner system of figured bass: three continuation lines.

⠼⠁⠃⠓ Twelve-eight time signature; found in headings, centered on a free line, at the beginning of a line, or between

⠆⠇ ⠶⠂ ⠶⠶

measures. In the latter case, a change of time signature is indicated. If one time signature is followed immediately by another, two time signatures are shown in print.

⠆⠇ ⠶⠂ ⠶⠶   1. When preceded and followed by a space: braille repeat; repeat the last thirteen measures.

2. In Spanner short-form scoring: thirteenth chord; follows the note name and rhythmic value.

⠆⠇ ⠶⠂ ⠶⠂ ⠶⠶   Braille repeat; repeat measures one through eight; a forward repeat that can be distinguished from the more common backward count repeat by the fact that the first number is smaller than the second. For backward count repeats, see ⠆⠇ ⠶⠶ ⠆⠇ ⠶⠶ , page 52.

⠆⠇ ⠶⠂ ⠆⠇ ⠶⠂ ⠶⠶   Braille repeat; repeat measures one through eight. Used in older transcriptions.

⠆⠇ ⠶⠶   1. At the margin: measure, staff, or rehearsal number two.

2. In the heading of music in section-by-section format: section two; subsequent sections of the music are numbered consecutively.

3. At the beginning of a paragraph of music: section two; subsequent sections of the music are numbered consecutively.

50   *In braille edition pages 66 and 67*

4. When preceded and followed by a space: braille repeat; repeat the last two measures. Any upper-cell number may be used according to the length of the passage to be repeated. If an octave sign precedes the number, the repeat should begin in the octave indicated.

5. Second ending sign; see ⠒⠂ , definition 3, page 49.

⠒⠂ ⠒⠂ ⠒⠂ Three-four time signature; found in headings, centered on a free line, at the beginning of a line, or between measures. In the latter case, a change of time signature is indicated. If one time signature is followed immediately by another, two time signatures were shown in the print.

⠒⠂ ⠒⠂ ⠒⠂ In the text of vocal music: braille repeat; a word or group of words should be repeated three times. The sign ⠒⠂ appears at the end of the word(s) to be repeated.

Example: ⠒⠂ ⠒⠂ ⠒⠂ ⠒⠂ ⠒⠂ ⠒⠂ ⠒⠂ ⠒⠂

The example indicates that the word *Amen* should be repeated three times (sung four times).

⠒⠂ ⠒⠂ 1. Marginal or heading number four.

2. At the beginning of a paragraph of music: section four.

3. When preceded and followed by a space: braille repeat; repeat the last four measures.

4. In Spanner short-form scoring: four chord or sus4. This follows the note name and rhythmic value. Example:

⠒⠂ ⠒⠂ ⠒⠂ is C4 or Csus4 with the duration of a whole note.

⠼⠙⠶ Four measures of rest. A number is used to indicate more than three consecutive measures of rest.

⠼⠙⠡ Change of key signature involving four natural signs. A number is used for more than three natural signs in a key signature or change of key signatures.

⠼⠙⠣ Key signature of four flats. A number is used in any key signature containing more than three flats.

⠼⠙⠩ Key signature of four sharps. A number is used in any key signature containing more than three sharps.

⠼⠙⠲ Four-four time signature; found in headings, centered on a free line, at the beginning of a line, or between measures. In the latter case, a change of time signature is indicated. If one time signature is followed immediately by another, two time signatures are shown in the print.

⠼⠙⠼⠃ 1. When preceded and followed by a space, braille repeat; count back four measures and repeat the first two. Any two unspaced upper-cell numbers should be read in this way. The first number locates the beginning of the repeat, and the second number specifies the length of the repeat. The repeat includes everything except a tie at the end of the last repeated measure. This form of repeat sign may be

52   *In braille edition pages 69 and 70*

preceded by an octave sign; if so, it indicates that the repeated measures begin in the new octave specified.

2. In music for electronic organ or harmonium: series of unspaced numbers giving the registration.

⠲ ⠖   1. Marginal or heading number six.

2. When preceded and followed by a space: braille repeat; repeat the last six measures.

3. In Spanner short-form scoring: sixth chord; follows the note name and rhythmic value. Example: ⠽ ⠬ ⠖   is a C sixth chord with the duration of a whole note.

⠆ ⠶   1. Marginal or heading number seven.

2. When preceded and followed by a space: braille repeat; repeat the last seven measures.

3. In Spanner short-form scoring: seventh chord; follows the note name and rhythmic value. Example: ⠆ ⠽ ⠶   is a C seventh chord with the duration of a whole note.

⠖ ⠶ ⠆ ⠶   In Spanner short-form scoring: seventh chord with flat ninth; follows the note name and rhythmic value.

⠆ ⠶ ⠲ ⠶ ⠲ ⠖ ⠆ ⠶   Braille repeat involving a page turn; this representative example means to count back eight bars and repeat the first seven of them. It also shows that a page turn occurs after the first three bars of that repeated passage.

In braille edition pages 70-72   53

⠿ ⠿ ⠿ ⠿

⠿ ⠿ ⠿ ⠿   Braille repeat; count back eight bars and repeat the first five of them. See ⠿ ⠿ ⠿ ⠿ , definition 1, page 52.

⠿ ⠿   1. Marginal or heading number nine.
2. When preceded and followed by a space: braille repeat; repeat the last nine measures. See ⠿ ⠿ , definition 4, page 51.
3. In Spanner short-form scoring: ninth chord; follows the note name and rhythmic value.

⠿ ⠿   Marginal indication that the music begins with an incomplete measure.

⠿ ⠿ ⠿   In Spanner short-form scoring: major seventh chord; follows the note name and rhythmic value.

⠿ ⠿ ⠿   In Spanner short-form scoring: flat five; follows the note name and rhythmic value.

⠿ ⠿ ⠿   In Spanner short-form scoring: flat nine; follows the note name and rhythmic value.

⠿ ⠿   1. Braille repeat; repeat measure one. Any lower-cell number when preceded and followed by a space indicates that a particular measure is repeated. When combined with another lower-cell number, it indicates a particular group of measures to be repeated. Example: ⠿ ⠿ ⠿ ⠿ means to

54   *In braille edition pages 72 and 73*

repeat measures one through eight. If the number sign is preceded by an octave sign, the repeat should begin in the new octave indicated. The repeat may also be modified by a dynamic sign appearing before the number sign.

2. First ending; distinguished from definition above by the absence of a space after the lower-cell numeral.

3. In the text of vocal music: verse one; a lower-cell number is sometimes used for the verse number.

4. At the beginning of a paragraph of music: staff number one; lower-cell numbers indicate the staves on each print page.

⠼⠢ ⠐ ⠌ ⠦ ⠒ Braille repeat; repeat measures one through four in the first section or staff of music. Other numbers may be used. The initial lower-cell number locates the section or staff, while the upper-cell numbers locate the measures to be repeated.

⠼⠢ ⠐ ⠦ ⠒ Braille repeat; repeat measures one through three. Other unspaced, lower-cell numbers have this meaning in older transcriptions.

⠼⠢ ⠐ ⠦ ⠒ Braille repeat; repeat measures one through eight. See ⠦ ⠒ , definition 1, page 54.

⠦ ⠒ 1. When preceded and followed by a space: braille repeat; repeat measure two. See ⠦ ⠒ , definition 1, page 54.

⠼⠃

2. When preceded by a space but followed immediately by music: second ending.

3. Following an in-accord sign: second verse or second part. Succeeding verses or parts will also be indicated with lower-cell numbers.

4. In Spanner system of figured bass: number two. See ⠼⠉ , definition 3, below.

⠼⠉ 1. When preceded and followed by a space: repeat measure three.

2. When preceded by a space but followed immediately by music: third ending.

3. In Spanner system of figured bass: number three; if modified by an accidental, the accidental appears between the numeral sign and the lower-cell number. Example: ⠼⠩⠉ . In this example, the number three is modified by a sharp. See figured bass, page 155.

⠼⠑ 1. When preceded and followed by a space: repeat measure five.

2. In Spanner system of figured bass: number five. See ⠼⠉ , definition 3, above.

⠼⠢⠔ In Spanner short-form scoring: augmented chord; follows the note name and rhythmic value. Example: ⠼⠈⠼⠢⠔ is a C augmented chord with the duration of a whole note.

⠿ ⠿ ⠿ ⠿   In Spanner short-form scoring: augmented seventh chord; follows the note name and rhythmic value.

⠿ ⠿ ⠿ ⠿   In Spanner short-form scoring: augmented ninth chord; follows the note name and rhythmic value.

⠿ ⠿   1. When preceded and followed by a space: repeat measure six.

2. In Spanner system of figured bass: number six. See ⠿ ⠿ , definition 3, page 56.

⠿ ⠿   1. When preceded and followed by a space: repeat measure seven.

2. In Spanner short-form scoring: diminished or diminished seventh chord; follows the note name and value. Example: ⠿ ⠿ ⠿   is a C diminished seventh chord with the duration of a whole note.

3. In Spanner system of figured bass: number seven. See ⠿ ⠿ , definition 3, page 56.

⠿ ⠿ ⠿ ⠿ ⠿   1. Repeat measures eight through sixteen. Other numbers used in the lower-cell position with a hyphen are read this way. See ⠿ ⠿ , definition 1, page 54.

2. In the heading of section-by-section music: measures eight through sixteen. Lower-cell numbers specify the measures included within a section. If either number is followed by dot 3, a measure at the beginning or the end of the section is incomplete.

In braille edition pages 76 and 77

⠿⠿

⠿⠿　In Spanner system of figured bass: number zero.

⠿⠿　In Spanner system of figured bass: short oblique line appearing in print under or above the preceding note.

⠿⠿　In Spanner system of figured bass: blank space in a column of figures. There may be two dot 3s or the dot 3 may follow a lower-cell number.

⠿⠿⠿　In Spanner system of figured bass: isolated natural sign. In print this appears under or above the preceding note.

⠿⠿⠿　In Spanner system of figured bass: isolated flat sign. In print this appears under or above the preceeding note.

⠿⠿⠿　In Spanner system of figured bass: isolated sharp sign. In print this appears under or above the preceding note.

⠿⠿　In Spanner system of figured bass: short oblique line passes through or above the lower-cell number that follows this sign.

⠿⠿⠿　In Spanner short-form scoring: chord with a lowered fifth; follows the note name and rhythmic value.

⠿　1. Word sign; literary abbreviation or dynamic marking follows. In some transcriptions, whole words may also follow.

　In braille edition pages 77 and 78

The music resumes when an octave sign or other music symbol appears.

   2. In the text of vocal music: end of the poetic line.

⠰⠁   1. In vocal music: alto voice.
   2. In instrumental music: *arpa* (harp).
   3. In accordion music: bass note A.
   4. In pre-1929 transcriptions: *a tempo*.

⠰⠁⠠ In accordion music: counterbass A.

⠁⠉ *Accelerando*.

⠁⠇ *Alto* (viola).

⠁⠎ *Assai*.

⠃   1. In vocal music: bass voice.
   2. In instrumental music: bassoon.
   3. In accordion music: bass note B.
   4. In pre-1929 transcription: *brillante*.

⠃⠠ In accordian music: counterbass B.

⠃⠃ Double bassoon (contra bassoon).

⠃⠃⠇ Bass clarinet.

In braille edition pages 78 and 79

⠿⠿ ⠿⠿ ⠿

⠿⠿⠿⠿ ⠿ Bass drum.

⠿⠿⠿⠿⠿ *Becken* (cymbals).

⠿⠿⠿⠿⠿ *Bass Klarinette* (bass clarinet).

⠿⠿⠿⠿ *Bratsche* (viola).

⠿⠿⠿⠿ In accordion music: bass solo.

⠿⠿⠿⠿⠿ Bass tuba.

⠿⠿ Beginning of *crescendo* (diverging) lines in print. These lines continue either until a new dynamic indication occurs or until the ending sign ⠿⠿ appears.

⠿⠿⠿ In accordion music: bass note C.

⠿⠿⠿⠿ In accordion music: counterbass C.

⠿⠿⠿⠿ *Cor anglais* (English horn).

⠿⠿⠿⠿ *Contrabasso* or *contrebasse* (double bass).

⠿⠿⠿⠿⠿ *Caisse claire* (snare drum).

⠿⠿⠿⠿⠿ In liturgical music: celebrant.

⠩ ⠩ ⠩ ⠩ ⠩   *Contrafagotto* (contra bassoon).

⠩ ⠩ ⠩ ⠩   Choir organ manual.

⠩ ⠩ ⠩ ⠩   *Corno inglese* (English horn).

⠩ ⠩ ⠩ ⠩   Clarinet.

⠩ ⠩ ⠩ ⠩ ⠩   First clarinet; any instrumental abbreviation may be followed by a lower-cell number to indicate first, second, or third part.

⠩ ⠩ ⠩ ⠩ ⠩ ⠩   First and second clarinet parts combined. The use of two lower-cell numbers indicates two parts.

⠩ ⠩ ⠩ ⠩   *Corno* (horn).

⠩ ⠩ ⠩ ⠩ ⠩   *Cor* (horn).

⠩ ⠩ ⠩ ⠩ ⠩   Cymbals.

⠩ ⠩   Beginning of *decrescendo* (converging) lines in print. These lines continue either until a new dynamic indication occurs or until the ending sign   ⠩ ⠩   appears.

⠩ ⠩ ⠩   In accordion music: bass note D.

In braille edition page 80

⠼⠗⠼⠗⠼⠗⠼⠗

⠼⠗⠼⠗⠼⠗⠼⠗ In accordion music: counterbass D.

⠼⠗⠼⠗⠼⠗⠼⠗ Double bass.

⠼⠗⠼⠗⠼⠗⠼⠗ *Da Capo;* return to the beginning of the piece or the movement.

⠼⠗⠼⠗⠼⠗⠼⠗ *Da Capo;* return to the beginning and play to the sign.

⠼⠗⠼⠗⠼⠗⠼⠗⠼⠗ *Da Capo;* return to the beginning and play eight measures. The number specifies the number of measures in the section to be repeated.

⠼⠗⠼⠗⠼⠗⠼⠗⠼⠗ *Doppel fagott.*

⠼⠗⠼⠗⠼⠗⠼⠗ Kettledrum.

⠼⠗⠼⠗⠼⠗⠼⠗ *Dal segno;* return to the *segno* or sign.

⠼⠗⠼⠗ In pre-1929 transcriptions: *espressivo.*

⠼⠗⠼⠗⠼⠗ In accordion music: bass note E.

⠼⠗⠼⠗⠼⠗⠼⠗ In accordion music: counter bass E.

⠼⠗⠼⠗⠼⠗⠼⠗⠼⠗⠼⠗ Echo organ manual.

⠿⠿⠿⠿ English horn.

⠿⠿⠿⠿⠿⠿ Illustrated or executed as follows.

⠿⠿⠿ In accordion music: bass note F.

⠿⠿⠿⠿ In accordion music: counterbass F.

⠿⠿⠿⠿ *Fagott* or *fagotto* (bassoon).

⠿⠿⠿⠿ Flute.

⠿⠿ 1. Great organ manual.
   2. In pre-1929 transcriptions: *gracioso*.

⠿⠿⠿ In accordion music: bass note G.

⠿⠿⠿⠿ In accordion music: counterbass G.

⠿⠿⠿⠿ *Gran cassa* (bass drum).

⠿⠿⠿ *Glissando.*

⠿⠿⠿⠿ 1. Great organ manual.
   2. *Grosse Trommel* (bass drum).

⠿⠿⠿ Harp.

⠿ ⠿ ⠿ ⠿

⠿ ⠿ ⠿ ⠿ *Hautbois* or *hoboe* (oboe).

⠿ ⠿ ⠿ ⠿ Horn.

⠿ ⠿ ⠿ First organ manual.

⠿ ⠿ ⠿ ⠿ Second organ manual.

⠿ ⠿ ⠿ ⠿ ⠿ Third organ manual.

⠿ ⠿ ⠿ ⠿ Fourth organ manual.

⠿ ⠿ *Arpeggio* for following chord. If preceded by dot 5, the chord is arpeggiated through both hands; if the second half of the sign is repeated, the *arpeggio* should be rolled in a downward direction.

⠿ ⠿ ⠿ ⠿ *Kontrabass* (double bass).

⠿ ⠿ ⠿ ⠿ ⠿ *Kleine Flöte* (piccolo).

⠿ ⠿ ⠿ *Arpeggio* in a downward direction.

⠿ ⠿ ⠿ ⠿ *Klarinette* (clarinet).

⠿ ⠿ ⠿ ⠿ *Kleine Trommel* (snare drum).

In braille edition pages 82 and 83

⠿⠿ In pre-1929 transcriptions: *legato.*

⠿⠿ *Molto.*

⠿⠿⠿ *Mezzo legato.*

⠿⠿⠿ *Mezzo voce.*

⠿⠿ 1. In harp music: use the fingernail.
   2. In pre-1929 transcriptions: *non.*

⠿⠿ For wind instruments: zero or circle over the next note.

⠿⠿⠿ Oboe.

⠿⠿⠿ In organ music: pedal keyboard (unusual).

⠿⠿⠿⠿ Piccolo.

⠿⠿⠿⠿⠿ *Petite flûte* (piccolo).

⠿⠿⠿⠿ *Piatti* (cymbal).

⠿⠿⠿⠿ *Pauken* (timpani).

In braille edition page 83   65

⠨⠏ ⠨⠕ ⠨⠎ ⠨⠮

⠨⠏ ⠨⠕ ⠨⠎ ⠨⠞ ⠨⠏ 1. Positif organ manual.
  2. *Posaune* (trombone).

⠨⠗ ⠨⠑ ⠨⠛ 1. In accordion music: register.
  2. In liturgical music: response.
  3. In organ music: *recit.*
  4. In pre-1929 transcriptions: *rallentando, ritardando,* or *ritenuto;* no distinction was made between different words.

⠨⠎ ⠨⠕ ⠨⠇ 1. In vocal music: soprano voice.
  2. In organ music: solo manual.
  3. In pre-1929 transcriptions: *sforzando.*

⠨⠎ ⠨⠊ ⠨⠙ ⠨⠗ ⠨⠍ Side drum.

⠨⠎ ⠨⠊ ⠨⠍ ⠨⠊ ⠨⠇ *Simile;* the passage should continue in the same manner; may refer to alternation of hands, use of pedal, or a distinctive pattern of nuances; it continues until a new hand, pedal, or nuance marking changes the pattern.

⠨⠎ ⠨⠕ ⠨⠇ ⠨⠕ ⠨⠛ Solo organ manual.

⠨⠎ ⠨⠑ ⠨⠝ ⠨⠽ In accordion music: *senza* register.

⠨⠎ ⠨⠕ ⠨⠞ ⠨⠞ *Sotto voce.*

⠨⠎ ⠨⠺ ⠨⠑ ⠨⠇ Swell organ manual.

In braille edition pages 83 and 84

⠒⠒ ⠒⠒ ⠒⠒ ⠒⠒   First soprano; any vocal part may be followed by a lower-cell number to indicate first, second, or third part.

⠒⠒ ⠒⠒ ⠒⠒ ⠒⠒ ⠒⠒   First and second soprano; the use of two lower-cell numbers indicates two parts.

⠒⠒ ⠒⠒ ⠒⠒   1. In vocal music: tenor.
   2. In pre-1929 transcriptions: *a tempo*.

⠒⠒ ⠒⠒ ⠒⠒ ⠒⠒   Trombone.

⠒⠒ ⠒⠒ ⠒⠒ ⠒⠒ ⠒⠒   *Tamburo militare* (snare drum).

⠒⠒ ⠒⠒ ⠒⠒ ⠒⠒ ⠒⠒   Timpani.

⠒⠒ ⠒⠒ ⠒⠒ ⠒⠒   Trumpet.

⠒⠒ ⠒⠒ ⠒⠒ ⠒⠒   *Tromba* (trumpet).

⠒⠒ ⠒⠒ ⠒⠒ ⠒⠒ ⠒⠒   Triangle.

⠒⠒ ⠒⠒ ⠒⠒ ⠒⠒   Tuba.

⠒⠒ ⠒⠒ ⠒⠒ ⠒⠒ ⠒⠒   In pre-1929 transcriptions: Tempo I or *a tempo*.

⠶⠶⠒⠂⠶⠶

⠶⠶⠒⠂⠶⠶ Unison; in the vertical score format, a unison of parts continues for four or more notes. It terminates when interval signs resume.

⠶⠶⠒⠂⠶⠶ 1. In instrumental music: violin.
2. In liturgical music: versicle.

⠶⠒⠂⠶⠶⠶⠶ Violoncello.

⠶⠶⠒⠂⠶⠶⠶⠶ Viola in some transcriptions and violin in other transcriptions. If *vl* is used for viola, *v* is used for violin; if *vl* is used for violin, *vla* is used for viola.

⠶⠶⠒⠂⠶⠶⠶⠶⠶⠶ Viola.

⠶⠶⠒⠂⠶⠶⠶⠶ First violin.

⠶⠶⠒⠂⠶⠶⠶⠶ Second violin.

⠶⠒⠂⠶⠶ 1. For wind instruments: cross or X appears over the next note.
2. In vocal music: half-spoken (*quasi parlando*). If written twice in succession, it is doubled for a series of notes.

⠶⠶⠒⠂⠶⠶ 1. In vertical score format: return to the original order and number of parts.
2. Indication for full chorus.

⠿ ⠒ ⠿ 1. In Canadian melody-chord system: paragraph indicator for the chorus part.

2. In vocal music: chorus.

⠿ ⠒ 1. In instrumental or keyboard music: pause or phrase. In print this is a comma, double short vertical lines between notes, or other similar device.

2. In vocal music: breath mark. According to Spanner, half breath; according to Reuss, full breath.

3. For Japanese koto: special plectrum symbol, *nami-gaeshi*.

4. In a keyboard passage for alternating hands: may represent the number one. See ⠿ ⠿ , definition 4, page 5.

⠿ ⠒ 1. Special plectrum symbol for Japanese instruments: *suriyubi* for samisen and *surizume* for koto.

2. In a keyboard passage for alternating hands: may represent the number two. See ⠿ ⠿ , definition 4, page 5.

⠿ ⠿ 1. End of the diverging lines for a *crescendo*.

2. In a keyboard passage for alternating hands: may represent the number three. See ⠿ ⠿ , definition 4, page 5.

⠿ ⠿ ⠿ Print music was written in the C (viola) clef.

⠿ ⠿ ⠒ ⠿ Print music was written with a C clef on the first line of the staff. Other lines of the staff are indicated by the

⠜⠲

appropriate octave mark in the third cell of this sign; i.e., the sign for second octave represents the second line of the staff, etc.

⠜⠲ 1. End of converging lines for a *decrescendo.*
2. In a keyboard passage for alternating hands: may represent the number four. See ⠃⠄ , definition 4, page 5.

⠜⠢ Asterisk; will be accompanied by a footnote. If there is more than one asterisk on the page, this sign will be followed immediately by a number or letter.

⠜⠢⠔ Asterisk; will be accompanied by a footnote. If there is more than one asterisk on the page, this sign will be followed immediately by a number or letter.

⠜⠖⠅ Print music was written in the bass (F) clef; used when the bass clef is in the right hand part.

⠜⠖⠇ Print music was written in the bass (F) clef.

⠜⠖⠄ Print music was written in the bass (F) clef.

⠜⠖⠸⠇ Print music was written in the bass clef placed on the third line of the staff; the octave sign in the third cell indicates the unusual placement. Other octave marks in that position indicate other lines of the staff. The sign for second octave represents the second line of the staff, etc.

⠰⠣ Beginning parenthesis; in some transcriptions all parenthetical expressions are preceded by the word sign. The sign ⠜ will indicate the close of the parentheses.

⠨⠣⠜ Print music was written in the treble (G) clef, used when the treble clef is in the left hand part.

⠨⠣⠜ Print music was written in the treble (G) clef.

⠰⠣⠔⠜ Asterisk surrounded by parentheses.

⠰⠣⠔⠣⠃⠜ Asterisk number one surrounded by parentheses.

⠰⠣⠜⠣⠃⠜ In music for plucked instruments: fret number one. Other fret numbers may appear. They will also be surrounded by parentheses and preceded by a word sign.

⠰⠣⠃⠜ Print music was written in the treble (G) clef.

⠨⠣⠁⠣ Print music was written in the treble (G) clef placed on the first line of the staff; the octave sign in the third cell of this sign indicates the unusual placement. Other octave signs in that position indicate other lines of the staff. The sign for second octave represents the second line of the staff, etc.

In braille edition pages 89 and 90

⠒⠒ ⠒⠒

⠒⠒ ⠒⠒   1. Print mark of interrogation or query; treated in the same way as an asterisk and accompanied by a footnote.

2. When followed by literary braille: opening parenthesis. The sign for the close of this parentheses is ⠒⠒ ⠒⠒ .

⠒⠒ ⠒⠒   1. In string music: the next note should be played in the fifth position or at the fifth fret; if preceded by dot 6, see ⠒⠒ ⠒⠒ ⠒⠒ , page 119.

2. In organ music: fifth (echo) manual. In some transcriptions this sign is preceded by dot 6, which does not alter the meaning.

⠒⠒ ⠒⠒ ⠒⠒   Print music was written in the C clef placed on the first line of the staff.

⠒⠒ ⠒⠒   1. In string music: the next note should be played in the sixth position or at the sixth fret; if preceded by dot 6, see ⠒⠒ ⠒⠒ ⠒⠒ , page 119.

2. Closing parenthesis. See ⠒⠒ ⠒⠒ .

⠒⠒ ⠒⠒ ⠒⠒   Print music was written in the C clef placed on the second line of the staff.

⠒⠒ ⠒⠒   1. In string music: the next note should be played in the second position or at the second fret; if preceded by dot 6, see ⠒⠒ ⠒⠒ ⠒⠒ , page 119.

In braille edition pages 90 and 91

2. In organ music: second (swell) manual. In some transcriptions this sign is preceded by dot 6, which does not alter the meaning.

⠩⠩⠇ Print music was written in the G clef; used when the music is to be played by the left hand or when the clef sign is placed on the lower (left hand) staff in print.

⠩⠩⠇ Print music was written in the G clef.

⠩⠩⠩⠇ Print music was written in the G clef placed on the first line of the staff. Other lines of the staff are indicated by the appropriate octave sign in the third cell of this sign. The sign for the third octave represents the third line of the staff, etc.

⠩⠩ 1. In string music: the next note should be played in the third position or at the third fret. If preceded by dot 6, see ⠩⠩⠩ , page 119.
2. In organ music: third (choir) manual. In some transcriptions this sign is preceded by dot 6, which does not alter its meaning.

⠩⠩⠇ Print music was written in the C clef.

⠩⠩⠩⠇ Print music was written in the C clef placed on the first line of the staff. Other lines of the staff are indicated by

⠒⠒ ⠒⠒

the appropriate octave sign in the third cell of this sign. The sign for the second octave represents the second line of the staff, etc.

⠒⠒ ⠒⠒ 1. In string music: the next note should be played in the fourth position or at the fourth fret. If preceded by dot 6, see ⠒⠒ ⠒⠒ ⠒⠒ , page 119.

2. In organ music: fourth (solo) manual. In some transcriptions this sign is preceded by dot 6, which does not alter its meaning.

⠒⠒ ⠒⠒ ⠒⠒ Print music was written in the F clef; used when the music is to be played by the right hand or when the clef sign is placed in the upper (right hand) staff.

⠒⠒ ⠒⠒ ⠒⠒ Print music was written in the F clef.

⠒⠒ ⠒⠒ ⠒⠒ ⠒⠒ Print music was written in the F clef placed on the third line of the staff. Other lines of the staff are indicated by the appropriate octave sign in the third cell of this sign; the sign for the fourth octave represents the fourth line, etc.

⠒⠒ ⠒⠒ 1. In string music: the next note should be played in the first position or at the first fret. If preceded by dot 6, see ⠒⠒ ⠒⠒ ⠒⠒ , page 119.

2. In organ music: first (great) manual. In some transcriptions this sign is preceded by dot 6, which does not alter its meaning.

3. In pre-1929 transcriptions: sign for *bouché* (closed).

⠶⠶⠶ Print music was written in the G clef placed on the first line of the staff.

⠶⠶⠶ In string music: the next note should be played in half position. If preceded by dot 6, see ⠶⠶⠶ , page 119.

⠶⠶ 1. End of a line of continuation; if there are two lines of continuation in effect, the end of the first one. The beginning of this line is indicated by the signs ⠶⠶ or ⠶⠶⠶ , according to different transcriptions.
   2. In figured bass: end of *tasto solo* section.
   3. In music for Japanese koto: special plectrum sign meaning *waren* for two string or *chirashizume* for one string.

⠶⠶⠶ Beginning of a line of continuation.

⠶⠶ 1. End of the second line of continuation. The beginning of this line is indicated by the signs ⠶⠶ or ⠶⠶⠶ according to different transcriptions.
   2. In string music: the next note should be played in the eighth position or at the eighth fret. If preceded by dot 6, see ⠶⠶⠶ , page 119.
3. In organ registration: minus sign.

⠶⠶⠶ Print music was written in the C clef placed on the fourth line of the staff.

In braille edition pages 93-95

⠿⠀⠿⠀⠿

⠿⠀⠿⠀⠿　In string music: the next note should be played in the twelfth position or at the twelfth fret. If preceded by dot 6, see ⠿ ⠿ ⠿ , page 119.

⠿⠀⠿⠀⠿　In string music: the next note should be played in the thirteenth position or at the thirteenth fret. If preceded by dot 6, see ⠿ ⠿ ⠿ , page 119.

⠿⠀⠿⠀⠿　In string music: the next note should be played in the ninth position or at the ninth fret. If preceded by dot 6, see ⠿ ⠿ ⠿ , page 119.

⠿⠀⠿⠀⠿　In string music: the next note should be played in the tenth position or at the tenth fret. If preceded by dot 6, see ⠿ ⠿ ⠿ , page 119.

⠿⠀⠿⠀⠿　In string music: the next note should be played in the eleventh position or at the eleventh fret. If preceded by dot 6, see ⠿ ⠿ ⠿ , page 119.

⠿⠀⠿⠀⠿　Beginning of a second line of continuation.

⠿⠀⠿⠀⠿⠀⠿　Print music was written in the treble (G) clef with an indication that the notes are to sound an octave lower than written.

⠿⠀⠿⠀⠿　End of a slur or line between staves. The beginning of this slur or line is marked ⠿ ⠿ .

⠮ ⠾ ⠮⠮ ⠾⠾ At this point a long slur enters a new staff and continues in effect.

⠮ ⠾ ⠮⠾ End of an oblique line between staves that shows a significant melodic progression. The beginning of this line is the sign ⠾ ⠮ .

⠮ ⠾ ⠮⠾ ⠾⠮ At this point a long phrasing slur enters a new staff and continues in effect.

⠮ ⠾ ⠾ Rehearsal letter A. Other rehearsal letters are also written with a word sign, an italic sign, and the letter.

⠮ ⠾ ⠿ ⠾ Print music was written in the treble (G) clef with an indication that notes are to sound an octave higher than written.

⠮ ⠾ ⠾ Print music was written in the C clef placed on the fifth line of the staff.

⠮ ⠾ ⠾ Print music was written in the F clef placed on the fifth line of the staff.

⠮ ⠾ ⠾ In organ music: abbreviation for *Positif*, which is capitalized to distinguish if from the dynamic *p*.

⠮ ⠾ ⠾ Opening of music parentheses. The closing of the parentheses is dots 6, 3.

In braille edition pages 96 and 97   77

⠆⠆

⠆⠆ 1. After a note: dotted note.

2. After a rest: dotted rest.

3. After an abbreviation: period.

4. After a marginal measure or staff number: that measure or staff is incomplete.

5. After a hand or part sign: separation of signs; used when the following braille character contains dots 1, 2, or 3. The sign is not always used in early transcriptions.

6. After a fingering sign in string music: beginning of a line of continuation for that fingering. The line ends when the finger sign is repeated and is preceded by dot 6.

7. After a fingering sign in keyboard music: omission of the second fingering in a series of alternative fingerings.

8. Between two consecutive repeat signs: indication that the repeats are not of equal value, and the second repeat is of longer duration.

9. In the text of vocal music: mute word syllable; the preceding syllable is not actually sung.

10. In organ music registration: prime sign, the symbol for foot. Example: ⠒⠂ ⠿⠒ ⠒⠂ equals ⠦⠆ ⠦⠖ ⠒⠆ ⠿⠦

11. In Spanner system of figured bass: blank space; used for alignment.

12. After an interval sign: note represented by that interval is a dotted note; occurs in a passage of moving notes. See ⠆⠂ , definition 7, page 114.

⠆⠂ ⠆⠆ 1. After a note: double dotted note.

2. After a rest: double dotted rest.

3. After an abbreviation such as *rit.* or *cresc.:* beginning of a line of continuation.

4. In sight method: prefix for words to distinguish them from notes that alternate on the same line. See sight method, page 140.

⠆⠆ ⠆⠆ ⠆⠆ 1. Triple dotted note or rest.

2. In the margin: the following line of music contains only an incomplete measure.

⠆⠆ ⠆⠆ ⠆⠆ ⠆⠆ ⠆⠆ In bar-over-bar music: tracker dots.

⠆⠆ 1. Interval of an octave; see intervals and chords, page 172. If written twice in succession, the sign is doubled.

2. In a melodic passage: tonal sequence. A repetition of the preceding melodic figure beginning on the pitch that immediately precedes this sign.

3. In RNIB chord symbols: the following letter is the counterbass and was underlined in print.

4. In the literal method of writing chord symbols: minus sign or hyphen; the two symbols are identical in print as well as in braille.

5. In modern figured bass notation: distinction of meanings. The preceding sign is a lower-cell number and the following sign has its regular musical meaning such as triplet, ornament, repeat, etc.

6. In chant notation: hyphen between two notes of the music indicating the point at which a change of word syllable

⠆⠆

occurs. Hyphens may also be found in the word line for syllabication. In the following illustration, the first syllable *pa-* is sung to three notes, and the final syllable *-trem* is sung to third octave A.

Example: ⠆⠆ ⠐⠆ ⠆⠆ ⠰⠆ ⠛⠆ ⠿⠆ ⠐⠆ ⠆⠆
⠆⠆ ⠐⠆ ⠆⠆ ⠛⠆ ⠿⠆ ⠐⠆ ⠰⠆ ⠆⠆

7. When preceded by a space: parallel motion at the interval of an octave. In a parallel type of format such as bar-over-bar, the notes in this part move parallel to the part on the line above at the distance of the interval indicated. In other formats, this part moves parallel to the preceding part. The distance between parts is not greater than one octave unless an octave sign precedes the parallel motion sign; if so, it indicates the octave in which to begin. If a parallel motion sign is followed immediately by a number, the number specifies the length of the passage of parallel motion. Example: ⠆⠆ ⠰⠆ ⠐⠆ means that the notes in this part move parallel to the notes in another part at the distance of one octave for the next four measures.

8. In organ registration: minus sign indicating the suppression of a stop.

9. In sight method: prefix for words; the hyphen precedes each uncapitalized word in order to distinguish words from music. In addition, hyphens may be used between words that are linked together rhythmically. See sight method, page 140.

10. In note-for-note method only: hyphen before a lower-cell sign indicating that the sign should *not* be read as a note

80   *In braille edition pages 99-101*

name in a chord. If method 2 is specified on the transcription, this is a staccato sign rather than a hyphen. See note-for-note, page 131.

⠦ ⠴ ⠒ 1. If preceded by a space: repeat measure one (or other number).

2. At top of page: may be the print page number or the running braille page number according to different usages.

⠦ ⠴ ⠒ ⠴ ⠲ ⠒ If preceded and followed by a space: repeat measures one through eight (or other numbers).

⠦ ⠴ ⠒ In accordion music: prefix for the part to be played by the left hand buttons.

⠦ ⠒ In a melodic passage: tonal sequence. A repetition of the preceding melodic figure beginning on the pitch that immediately precedes this sign. In the print copy these notes were written out.

⠦ ⠒ 1. Following a note: doubled octave interval sign.

2. Following an abbreviation such as *rit.* or *cresc.*: line of continuation. This is the second line of continuation in effect during the passage.

3. In the text of Anglican chant: asterisk or breath mark.

⠒ 1. First octave; affects the note, interval, repeat, or parallel motion sign that follows immediately. The first

⠆⠒

octave begins on the lowest C on the piano keyboard and goes up through the next B above. If a note or a repeat is preceded by two different octave signs, use the second sign for the performance. See 8ba, ⠦⠒ , definition 1, page 105.

2. In accordion music: first row of buttons.

3. For bowed string instruments: artificial harmonic; applies to the following note or interval which is shown in print as diamond-shaped. This sign precedes an accidental or an octave sign for the braille note.

4. For plucked instruments: little or optional *barré* if it precedes a fret sign; bass note if it precedes a string sign.

5. In the text of vocal music: accent mark. In English used before a syllable that otherwise would not be pronounced separately. Example: *blessed* is sung on one note, but *bless'ed* requires a note for the final syllable. In foreign languages, used before accented letters.

6. In Japanese music for shakuhachi: the next note should be played with the special *shakuhachi* sound.

7. In the Rodenberg system of harmonic analysis: indication of an augmented chord; placed between the letter sign and number sign of a roman numeral. Example: ⠆⠒ ⠰⠒ ⠒⠆ ⠒⠒   is an augmented III chord.

8. In the text of chant music: stress mark; found immediately before the word or syllable to be stressed.

9. In vertical score format keyboard music: shows the division of a chord between hands; the interval(s) following this sign should be played by the right hand. In the organ

82   *In braille edition pages 102-104*

accompaniment for chant notation (vertical score format), there may be notes rather than intervals following this sign. These notes should be played by the right hand; in this case, dot 4 acts as an in-accord sign.

10. In vertical score format vocal music: indication that the next interval should be read downward. (That voice crosses below the previous voice.)

⠿ ⠿ 1. Slur; used with grace notes or notes in small type. (It does not have this meaning in United States transcriptions.) See definitions 2, 3, and 4.

2. In vocal music: *portamento;* placed between notes.

3. In instrumental or keyboard music: *glissando;* placed between notes.

4. In music for plucked instruments: *glissando,* change of position with finger lightly touching string, or slide from string to string according to the context of the music.

⠿ ⠿ ⠿ ⠿ Downward *glissando* following a note.

⠿ ⠿ End of a square bracket above the staff.

⠿ ⠿ 1. Following a note; tie; sometimes used when a note is to be held or allowed to ring even though the tied note does not appear again. (Braille follows print usage.)

2. Following an interval: the particular note of the chord represented by that interval is tied.

⠒⠒ ⠒⠒ ⠒⠒

3. At the beginning of a line: reminder tie.

4. In vocal music: tie or *portamento* according to context. If the preceding and following pitches are the same, a tie; if different, a *portamento*.

⠒⠒ ⠒⠒ ⠒⠒   Doubled form of the tie sign.

⠒⠒ ⠒⠒ ⠶⠶   Repeat that begins with a tie.

⠒⠒ ⠶⠶   1. In organ pedal part: foot crosses in front.

2. In music for Japanese instruments: *ato-oshi* for koto and *suriage* for samisen (press the string with left hand).

⠒⠒ ⠶⠶   In guitar music: first finger of the right hand; precedes note to be plucked.

⠒⠒ ⠦⠴ ⠴⠦   In string music: down bow at the frog of the bow.

⠒⠒ ⠒⠒   If immediately followed by a value sign: prefix for passage of music written in the substitution method; lowest note of the passage is in the first octave. See   ⠔⠶ ⠒⠒ ⠒⠒   , page 93.

⠒⠒ ⠴⠦   Half slur. In a long slur in print, this is the point where the slur is bent into an angle to signify slight phrasing; it then continues as a slur.

84

⠒⠂ ⠒⠢ Ornament; descending print curve preceding a note, usually indicating an upper grace note.

⠒⠂ ⠒⠆ 1. In music for Japanese instruments: *hajiki* for samisen and *hajikizume* for koto (left hand *pizzicato*); applies to the following note.
   2. In string music: semi-staccato bow stroke.
   3. In keyboard music: a small *v* under or above the next note.

⠒⠂ ⠒⠆ ⠒⠂ In guitar music: *rasgueado* up with the index finger.

⠒⠂ ⠒⠆ ⠒⠆ In guitar music: *rasgueado* up with the middle finger.

⠒⠂ ⠒⠆ ⠒⠢ In guitar music: *rasgueado* up with the thumb.

⠒⠂ ⠒⠆ ⠒⠢ In guitar music: *rasgueado* up with the ring finger.

⠒⠂ ⠒⠆ ⠒⠆ ⠒⠆ ⠒⠆ Ornament; *Bebung*. In print this is a curve over dots placed above a note; the number of dots in the print regulates the number of staccato marks in the braille sign. See also ⠆⠂ ⠒⠂ ⠒⠂ ⠒⠂ ⠒⠂ , page 23.

⠒⠂ ⠒⠰ If preceded by a space: braille repeat beginning in first octave; the following upper- or lower-cell numeral indicates which measure or group of measures should be repeated.

In braille edition pages 106 and 107

⠂⠂ ⠐⠂

⠂⠂ ⠐⠂ 1. In organ music: *senza* pedal.

2. In music for Japanese koto or samisen: special plectrum sign, *otoshi*; precedes the note.

3. Marginal indication: highest voice of the ensemble.

⠂⠂ ⠂⠂ Below the first octave; affects the note, interval, or repeat sign that follows. On the piano keyboard notes below the first octave are to the left of the lowest C.

⠂⠂ ⠂⠂ ⠐⠂ End of a square bracket above the staff that was indicated in print with a broken line; usually the second set of brackets for a passage.

⠂⠂ ⠐⠂ ⠐⠂ Ornament; long (extended) inverted (upper) mordent beginning with a turn.

⠐⠂ 1. Second octave; affects the note, interval, repeat, or parallel motion sign that follows immediately. The second octave begins on the C that is two octaves below middle C and goes up through the next B above. If a note or repeat is preceded by two different octave signs, the second sign is used for performance. See 8ba ⠐⠂ , definition 1, page 105.

2. For accordion: second row of buttons.

3. For plucked instruments: half *barré* if it precedes a fret sign; *acorde* (chord) if it precedes a string sign.

4. In organ registration: the following stop also applies to the pedal keyboard.

⠒⠂⠒⠂ 1. The preceding note or chord should be divided and performed as quarter notes. Example: ⠒⠂⠒⠆⠒⠂⠒⠂ equals ⠒⠂⠒⠆⠒⠆⠒⠆⠒⠆ .

2. Beginning of a square bracket above the staff.

⠒⠂⠒⠂⠒⠂ 1. Doubled form of the above sign; indicates a series of notes or chords that should be divided into quarter notes.

2. Beginning of a square bracket above the staff that was indicated in print with a broken line; generally used to differentiate between two sets of square brackets that may overlap.

⠒⠂⠒⠆ The preceding note or chord should be divided and performed as eighth notes. Example: ⠒⠂⠒⠆⠒⠂⠒⠆ equals ⠒⠂⠒⠂⠒⠂⠒⠆⠒⠆⠒⠆ . When this sign is doubled, only the second half of the sign is written twice. Example: ⠒⠆⠒⠂⠒⠆⠒⠂ .

⠒⠂⠒⠒ 1. Accumulating *arpeggio;* the preceding note and the single notes that follow this sign are all tied over to the next chord.

2. In pre-1929 transcriptions: tie for a note or for one interval of a chord.

3. Between two identical whole notes: double whole note.

4. Between two whole rests: double whole rest.

⠒⠂⠒⠆ The preceding note or chord should be divided and performed as 64th notes. When this sign is doubled, only the second half of the sign is written twice. Example: ⠒⠆⠒⠂⠒⠆⠒⠆ .

In braille edition pages 109 and 110   87

⠒⠆

⠒⠆ The preceding note or chord should be divided and performed as 16th notes. Example: ⠼⠆ ⠒⠆ ⠒⠆ ⠒⠆ equals ⠒⠆ ⠒⠆ ⠒⠆ ⠒⠆ ⠒⠆ . When this sign is doubled, only the second half of the sign is written twice. Example: ⠒⠆ ⠒⠆ ⠒⠆ ⠒⠆ .

⠒⠆ ⠆⠆ ⠒⠆ Distinction of rhythmic values (larger); the following note or notes are whole notes, half notes, quarter notes, or eighth notes; applies to rests as well as notes.

⠒⠆ ⠒⠆ If immediately followed by a value sign: prefix for passage of music written in the substitution method; lowest note of the passage is in the second octave. See ⠒⠆ ⠒⠆ ⠒⠆ , page 93.

⠒⠆ ⠒⠆ 1. The preceding note or chord should be divided and performed as a *tremolo* or as 32nd notes. When this sign is doubled, only the second half of the sign is written twice. Example: ⠒⠆ ⠒⠆ ⠒⠆ ⠒⠆ .

2. In percussion music: roll; for example, a drum roll or a roll on the cymbals.

⠒⠆ ⠒⠆ 1. In instrumental music: end of slur (braille terms: long or bracket slur).

2. In vocal music: end of a phrasing slur.

⠒⠆ ⠒⠆ 1. In music for bowed instruments: left hand *pizzicato* on next note. (According to Reuss, *Index à la Notation*

⠶ ⠦ ⠴ *Musical Braille*, 1966.) See definition 2 and select the meaning according to the context of the music.

2. In music for bowed instruments: *arco* on next note. (According to Nemeth, *Dictionary of Braille Music Symbols* 1953.) See definition 1 and select the meaning according to the context of the music.

3. In music for Japanese samisen: *urahajiki* on the following note; put a finger of the left hand at the neck of the samisen and pluck the string with that finger.

⠆ ⠖ ⠴ 1. In music for bowed instruments: left hand *pizzicato* with the first finger.

2. In guitar music: *rasgueado* downward with the index finger.

⠒ ⠖ ⠂ 1. In music for bowed instruments: left hand *pizzicato* with the second finger.

2. In guitar music: *rasgueado* downward with the middle finger.

⠢ ⠖ ⠂ In guitar music: *rasgueado* downward with the thumb.

⠲ ⠖ ⠢ 1. In music for bowed instruments: left hand *pizzicato* with the third finger.

2. In guitar music: *rasgueado* downward with the ring finger.

In braille edition pages 112 and 113

⠇⠃⠶ ⠇⠃⠶ ⠇⠃⠶

⠇⠃⠶ ⠇⠃⠶ ⠇⠃⠶   In music for bowed instruments: left hand *pizzicato* with the fourth finger.

⠇⠃ ⠇⠃   If preceded by a space: braille repeat beginning in second octave; the following upper or lower-cell number indicates which measure or group of measures should be repeated beginning in the second octave.

⠇⠃ ⠇⠃   1. Prefix for organ pedal part.
   2. Marginal indication: second highest voice of the vocal or instrumental ensemble.

⠇⠃ ⠆⠃   The preceding note or chord should be divided and performed as 128th notes. When this sign is doubled, only the second half of the sign (dot 3) is written twice.

⠇⠃   1. Third octave; affects the note, interval, repeat, or parallel motion sign that follows immediately. The third octave begins on the C one octave below middle C, and it goes up to, but does not include, middle C. If a note or repeat is preceded by two different octave signs, the second sign is used for performance. See 8va, ⠇⠃ , definition 1, page 105.
   2. Punctuation indicator; separates a music symbol from any punctuation mark except the comma, which is represented by dot 6.
   3. For accordion: third row of buttons.
   4. For plucked instruments: grand *barré;* precedes the fret sign.

90

5. In organ registration: the following registration applies to both hands and to the pedal part.

⠐⠦ 1. The preceding note has a quarter stem in addition to the rhythmic value shown with the note itself. This stem may be dotted (if followed by dot 3), and it may be modified with a staccato, accent, slur, or tie.

2. In music of indefinite pitch such as percussion music: quarter note.

3. In Spanner system of figured bass: the preceding figure or column of figures has the duration of a quarter note.

⠸⠦ 1. The preceding note has an eighth stem in addition to the rhythmic value shown with the note itself; stem may be dotted (if followed by dot 3), and it may be modified with a staccato, accent, slur, or tie.

2. In music of indefinite pitch such as percussion music: eighth note.

3. In Spanner system of figured bass: the preceding figure or column of figures has the duration of an eighth note.

⠸⠴ 1. In a heading: *alla breve* or cut time (time signature).

2. In keyboard music: slur passing from one in-accord part to another in the same staff or from one hand to another. In some transcriptions (especially Italian braille), the end of a long phrasing slur.

3. In vocal music: syllabic slur that applies to one verse only or to one language only.

⠒⠒ ⠒⠒ ⠒⠒

⠒⠒ ⠒⠒ ⠒⠒ In keyboard music: slur of three or more notes passing from one in-accord part to another in the same staff or from one hand to the other. In some transcriptions (especially Italian braille), the beginning of a long slur.

⠒⠒ ⠒⠒ 1. The preceding note has a half-note stem in addition to the rhythmic value shown with the note itself; stem may be dotted (if followed by dot 3), and may be modified with a staccato, accent, slur, or tie.

2. In music of indefinite pitch such as percussion music: half note.

3. In Spanner system of figured bass: the preceding figure or column of figures has half note value.

⠒⠒ ⠒⠒ 1. The preceding note has a 16th stem in addition to the value shown with the note itself; stem may be dotted (if followed by dot 3), and may be modified with a staccato, accent, slur, or tie.

2. In music of indefinite pitch such as percussion music: 16th note.

⠒⠒ ⠒⠒ Ornament; inverted *v* between two adjacent notes in print.

⠒⠒ ⠒⠒ ⠒⠒ In keyboard music: half pedal up.

⠒⠒ ⠒⠒ ⠒⠒ In string music: down bow in the middle portion of the bow.

⠒⠿⠒ In keyboard music: half pedal down.

⠰⠿⠆ 1. Pause or *fermata* on a bar line. See definition 2.
2. *Fine* bar line.

⠆⠿⠰ In string music: up bow in the middle portion of the bow.

⠰⠶⠆ Prefix for passage of music written in the substitution method; lowest note of the passage is in the third octave and every note is a 16th. Substitution is an alternate method of writing music containing frequent octave changes. The prefix for a passage of substitution always consists of three cells. The first is an octave sign indicating the lowest octave of the passage; the second is ⠶ ; the third indicates the rhythmic value of each note in the passage. The rhythmic values are as follows:

⠐ quarter notes
⠨ eighth notes
⠰ 16th notes
⠠ 32nd notes
⠈ 64th notes

Since the rhythmic value has been established in the prefix, dots 3 and 6 of each note specify the octave. There are no more than four different octaves within the passage; these are illustrated in the following example with the note C.

⠰ lowest octave of passage
⠘ second highest octave of passage

⠰⠒ ⠂

⠒⠒ third highest octave of passage
⠒⠒ fourth highest octave of passage

The first line of the following example is one measure of music in the substitution method. The second line of the example is the same measure written without the substitution method.

⠒⠒⠒⠒⠒⠒⠒⠒⠒⠒⠒⠒⠒⠒⠒⠒⠒⠒

⠒⠒⠒⠒⠒⠒⠒⠒⠒⠒⠒⠒⠒⠒⠒⠒⠒⠒⠒⠒⠒⠒⠒⠒

⠒⠒ ⠒⠒   1. The preceding note has a 32nd stem in addition to the value shown with the note itself; stem may be dotted (if followed by dot 3) and may be modified with a staccato, accent, slur, or tie.

2. In music of indefinite pitch such as percussion music: 32nd note.

⠒⠒ ⠒⠒ ⠒⠒   Beginning of a rhythmic group of two notes. The number of notes in such groups is shown by the middle character, a number in lower-cell position. Example:
⠒⠒ ⠒⠒ ⠒⠒ ⠒⠒   indicates a rhythmic group of ten notes. This sign may be doubled for a series of rhythmic groups. Example: ⠒⠒ ⠒⠒ ⠒⠒ ⠒⠒ ⠒⠒ .

⠒⠒ ⠒⠒ ⠒⠒   Triplet within a triplet or a rhythmic group of three notes. The doubled form of this sign is ⠒⠒ ⠒⠒ ⠒⠒ ⠒⠒ ⠒⠒
See ⠒⠒ ⠒⠒ ⠒⠒ .

⠒⠒ ⠒⠒   Ornament; grace note preceded by an ascending curve.

In braille edition pages 118-120

⠿⠿⠿ Rhythmic group of five notes begins. The doubled form of the sign is ⠿⠿⠿⠿⠿ . See ⠿⠿⠿ .

⠿⠿⠿ Rhythmic group of six notes begins. The doubled form of this sign is ⠿⠿⠿⠿⠿ . See ⠿⠿⠿ .

⠿⠿ 1. Short line above or below the following note indicating an *agogic* accent; *tenuto*.

2. In chant notation: prefix for *mora vocis*, a slight *tenuto* or retardation.

⠿⠿⠿ Rhythmic group of eight notes begins here. The doubled form of this sign is ⠿⠿⠿⠿⠿ . See ⠿⠿⠿ .

⠿⠿ In the note-for-note method 2 only: ornament; turn shown above the note in print.

⠿⠿ If preceded by a space: braille repeat beginning in third octave; the following upper or lower-cell number indicates which measure or group of measures is repeated.

⠿⠿ 1. Prefix for left hand keyboard part.
2. In string music: left hand *pizzicato*.
3. In margin: third highest voice of an ensemble.

⠿⠿⠿ In keyboard music: the following notes should be played by the left hand with the intervals reading down.

⠒⠒ ⠒⠒

⠒⠒ ⠒⠒   1. The preceding note is shown as a whole note in addition to the value shown with the note itself; whole note may be dotted (if followed by dot 3) and may be modified with an accent, slur, or tie.

2. In music of indefinite pitch such as percussion music: whole note.

3. In Spanner system of figured bass: whole note value for the preceding figure or column of figures.

⠒⠒ ⠒⠒ In the note-for-note method 2 only: *tenuto* or *agogic* accent.

⠒⠒   1. Fourth octave; affects the note, interval, repeat, or parallel motion sign that follows immediately. The fourth octave begins on middle C and includes all the notes up through the next B above. If a note or repeat is preceded by two different octave signs, use the second sign for performance. See 8va, ⠒⠒ , definition 1, page 105.

2. Prefix to designate a sign that does not appear in print but has been added to clarify the braille transcription; may be found before rests, accidentals, dynamic indications, and other abbreviations in facsimile braille transcriptions.

3. At the end of a line or followed by a space: music hyphen.

4. For accordion: fourth row of buttons.

5. In chant notation: used for pointing the text; follows a group syllables that are to be sung on the previous note, and

separates these from the syllables to be sung on the following note.

⠿ ⠿ 1. Short line or slur drawn between the print staves to show that a particular melodic line moves from one hand to the other. In simple music this sign is shown only where the line leaves the first part; in complex music it is also found where the line enters the second part.

2. In pre-1954 transcriptions: sometimes used to indicate that a chord or note should continue to ring or to vibrate.

⠿ ⠿ ⠿ Long slur that transfers from one hand to the other.

⠿ ⠿ ⠿ Ornament; in print a short, thick line between two adjacent notes.

⠿ ⠿ ⠿ Termination of a line (or slur) between hands; found only where there could be confusion concerning the beginning and the end of the line.

⠿ ⠿ 1. In string music: natural harmonic on the preceding note.

2. In music for Japanese instruments: *hiki-iro* for koto and *surisage* for samisen (loosen string).

⠿ ⠿ 1. In keyboard music: oblique line between staves that indicates a significant melodic progression.

⠒⠂ ⠒⠂ ⠒⠂

2. In guitar music: middle finger of right hand; precedes note to be plucked.

⠒⠂ ⠒⠂ ⠒⠂ In keyboard music: release the pedal slowly.

⠒⠂ ⠒⠂ ⠒⠂ In string music: down bow at the point of the bow.

⠒⠂ ⠒⠂ ⠒⠂ In keyboard music: half pedal or lower the pedal slowly.

⠒⠂ ⠒⠂ ⠒⠂ Pause, hold, or *fermata* placed between two notes.

⠒⠂ ⠒⠂ ⠒⠂ In music for Japanese samisen: *urabachi* (*bachi* turned over) for next note.

⠒⠂ ⠒⠂ If immediately followed by a value sign: prefix for a passage of music written in the substitution method; lowest note of the passage is in the fourth octave. See ⠒⠂ ⠒⠂ ⠒⠂ , page 93.

⠒⠂ ⠒⠂ 1. Part-measure in-accord; connects sections of music that in print are written vertically rather than horizontally. Each section of music so connected has the same number of rhythmic beats and, in most instances, is only part of the total number of beats in the measure. Part-measure in-accords are separated from the rest of the measure by ⠒⠂ ⠒⠂ . See in-accords, page 169.

98

2. Whole-measure in-accord. When the section sign ⠰⠆ is not present, this in-accord applies to the whole measure.

⠆ ⠒ 1. End of a square bracket above the staff.

2. In pre-1929 transcriptions: beginning of a *crescendo* indicated by diverging lines.

⠆ ⠖ 1. When preceded by a space: print page turn; may stand alone or be followed by the number of the next print page. An unusual use occurs when the print pagination sign is preceded by a number (with its numeral prefix) and followed by another number without a numeral prefix; the first number tells how many measures are to be repeated before the page turn, and the second number tells how many more measures are in this repeat after the page turn. See also ⠶⠆⠶⠒⠒⠖⠖⠒ , page 53.

2. In organ pedal part: crossing of foot in front; precedes the note to be played by the crossing foot.

3. In the note-for-note method 2 only: ornament; inverted (upper) mordent.

⠆ ⠖ ⠒ In the note-for-note method 2 only: ornament; mordent (lower mordent).

⠆ ⠖ Ornament; mordent (lower mordent) that was placed below a turn in print.

⠒⠒ ⠶⠶ ⠒⠒

⠒⠒ ⠒⠶ ⠒⠒ Ornament; print shows an upward curve preceding a turn.

⠒⠒ ⠒⠶ Ornament; the following note with any intervals it may have is an *appoggiatura*; in print, a grace note with no cross stroke.

⠒⠶ ⠒⠒ Ornament; inverted (upper) mordent beginning on the note or interval that follows. Fingering, if given, will follow that note or interval sign.

⠒⠶ ⠒⠒ ⠒⠂ Ornament; mordent (lower mordent) beginning on the note or interval that follows. Fingering, if given, follows that note or interval sign.

⠒⠶ ⠒⠒ 1. The following note or interval is semi-staccato; in print a line and a dot above or below a note. If written twice in succession, it is doubled for a series of nuances.

2. In the words of chant music: the following words should be sung on the reciting note; the sign ⠶⠶ ⠒⠒ marks the end of this group of words.

⠒⠂ ⠒⠒ When preceded by a space: *dal segno* or *D.S.;* return to the *segno* ⠒⠂ in the music. This sign may be followed immediately by a letter to indicate *segno* A, *segno* B, etc.

⠒⠂ ⠒⠒ ⠒⠒ ⠒⠒ ⠶⠶ Preceded and followed by a space: braille *dal segno* or *D.S.;* return to *segno* A and play three measures.

In braille edition pages 126 and 127

Subsequent *dal segnos* will be lettered B, C, etc. The final number always indicates the number of measures in the section to be repeated.

⠶ ⠦ ⠴ Braille *coda* sign; go to the *coda* section of the music.

⠶ ⠦ ⠆ When preceded by a space: braille *dal segno;* return to the *segno* and play or sing the passage ending with the sign ⠦

⠶ ⠆ When preceded by a space: braille repeat beginning in fourth octave; the following upper or lower-cell number indicates which measure or group of measures is repeated beginning in the fourth octave.

⠶ ⠆ 1. Designation of the solo voice part. In bar-over-bar format with piano accompaniment, usually an outline containing only the notes, rests, and ties of the solo part.
2. Marginal indication for the fourth highest voice of an ensemble.

⠶ ⠦ ⠴ The following chord is arpeggiated through two or more staves.

⠶ ⠦ ⠴ ⠴ The following chord is arpeggiated in a downward direction through two or more staves.

In braille edition pages 127 and 128   101

⠆⠆ ⠒⠒

⠒⠒ ⠒⠒ In the note-for-note method 2 only: semi-staccato.

⠆⠆ ⠒⠒ ⠆⠆ Transfer of a phrasing slur between staves. The phrase continues.

⠒⠒ 1. Fifth octave; affects the note, interval, repeat, or parallel motion sign that follows immediately. The fifth octave begins on the C that is one octave above middle C, and it goes up through the next B above. If a note or repeat is preceded by two different octave signs, use the second sign for performance. See 8va, ⠰⠆ , definition 1, page 105.

2. For accordion: fifth row of buttons.

3. In Spanner system of figured bass: the following accidental stands alone in print; not associated with a numerical figure.

4. In the text of chant notation: italics to indicate stress.

⠆⠆ ⠒⠒ 1. Alternation in 64ths; appears between the notes or chords to be alternated.

2. In string music: thumb sign in early transcriptions.

⠆⠆ ⠒⠒ ⠆⠆ In organ music: first manual.

⠆⠆ ⠰⠆ Alternation in eighths; appears between the notes or chords to be alternated.

⠆⠆ ⠰⠆ ⠆⠆ In organ music: second manual.

102

⠰⠄ ⠦⠆   1. In a heading: time signature represented by C in print.

2. Following a chord: chord tie; used when two or more notes of the chord are tied or when the chord should be allowed to ring, even though the tied notes do not appear again. (Braille follows print usage.)

3. In pre-1954 transcriptions: may be used for an accumulating *arpeggio* as well as a tie.

⠰⠄ ⠦⠆ ⠦⠆   The doubled form of the chord tie; the next four or more chords contain at least two notes that are tied over from one chord to the next.

⠰⠆ ⠰⠆   Measure division or section; indicates the end or the beginning of a part-measure in-accord. See in-accords, page 169.

⠰⠆ ⠰⠆   Alternation in 16ths; appears between the notes or chords to be alternated.

⠰⠆ ⠦⠆ ⠰⠆   In organ music: third manual.

⠰⠆ ⠰⠰   Ornament; V between two adjacent notes.

⠰⠄ ⠦⠆   If immediately followed by a value sign: prefix for passage of music written in the substitution method; lowest note of the passage is in the fifth octave. See   ⠰⠄ ⠦⠆ ⠰⠆ , page 93.

⠒⠒ ⠒⠒

⠒⠒ ⠒⠒ Alternation in 32nds or as *tremolo;* appears between the notes or chords to be alternated.

⠒⠒ ⠒⠒ ⠒⠒ In organ music: fourth manual.

⠒⠒ ⠒⠒ 1. Ornament; grace note preceded by a descending curve.

2. In Canadian melody-chord system: rhythm sign. The doubled form of the sign is ⠒⠒ ⠒⠒ ⠒⠒ . Indicates that the following note(s) are not sung but are applied to a spoken or percussive passage.

⠒⠒ ⠒⠒ 1. The next note or interval has an accent; in print a thin horizontal V above or below a note. If repeated immediately, the sign is doubled for a series of accents.

2. In chant notation: *ictus* or short vertical line under the following note; indicates rhythmic grouping.

⠒⠒ ⠒⠒ When preceded by a space: braille repeat beginning in fifth octave; the following upper or lower-cell number indicates which measure or group of measures is repeated.

⠒⠒ ⠒⠒ 1. Prefix for right hand keyboard part.

2. Marginal indication for the fifth highest voice of an ensemble.

⠒⠒ ⠒⠒ ⠒⠒ In keyboard music: the following notes should be played by the right hand with the intervals reading up.

104   *In braille edition pages 130 and 131*

⠨⠄ Alternation in 128ths; appears between the notes or chords to be alternated.

⠨⠤ In the note-for-note method 2 only: accent.

⠨⠸⠉ Slur; the end of a slur moving from one in-accord part to another.

⠨⠐⠉ Slur; the end of a slur extending from one staff to another.

⠨⠐⠇ The end of an oblique line between staves.

⠨⠰⠃ Slur; the continuation of a phrasing slur that began in the adjacent staff.

⠰ 1. Sixth octaves; affects the note, interval, repeat, or parallel motion sign that follows immediately. The sixth octave begins on the C that is two octaves above middle C, and goes up through the next B above. Occasionally the music has two different octave signs written consecutively. This occurs because the print music is written in one octave on the staff with an 8ba, or 8va, or other indication that the performance is intended for a higher or lower octave. In braille the first octave sign represents the location on the print staff, and the second octave sign is the pitch intended for performance.

2. For accordion: sixth row of buttons.

3. In Spanner system of figured bass: an oblique stroke accompanies the number that follows; shown in print either above or through that number.

4. In Rodenberg system of harmonic analysis: letter sign preceding a number sign indicating a roman numeral. See ⠒⠒ , definition 2, page 112.

5. In neumatic notation: the separation between neumes or termination of a neume.

6. Double moving-note sign. When this sign appears between two sets of interval signs, those sets of intervals move while the remainder of the chord is stationary. The moving intervals receive equal time value. The following example should be read up. The first line has moving notes, and the second line is the same measure written with an in-accord.

Example:

Also see ⠢ , definition 7, page 114.

In English chord-symbol system: A major.

1. In instrumental and keyboard music: beginning of phrasing slur (braille terms: long or bracket slur).

2. In vocal music: phrasing slur (as distinguished from a syllabic slur).

In braille edition pages 133 and 134

3. In English chord-symbol system: B major.

⠦⠴ ⠦⠴ ⠦⠴ ⠦⠴   Phrasing slur; one slur ends and another begins on the following note.

⠦⠦   1. Special short slur for a grace note; not always used for grace notes, and performance does not vary between this slur sign and the sign ⠉⠉ . See definition 2.

2. Slur; at the beginning of a new section, continuation of slur from previous section. Within a paragraph of music, slur that ends on a bar, double bar, or rest. Select meaning from context of music.

3. In English chord-symbol system: C major.

4. In pre-1954 transcriptions of keyboard music: slur that moves from one hand part to another.

⠴⠲   In English chord-symbol system: D major.

⠴⠢   In English chord-symbol system: E major.

⠴⠦   In English chord-symbol system: F major.

⠦⠴   In English chord-symbol system: G major.

⠦⠴   1. In English chord-symbol system: A minor.

2. In music for Japanese koto or samisen: *yuri* (with the left hand alternately press down and free the string a few times at the left side of the bridge).

In braille edition pages 134 and 135   107

⠆⠆ ⠆⠆

⠆⠆ ⠆⠆   1. In English chord-symbol system: B minor.
   2. In guitar music: pluck the next note with the ring finger of the right hand; the print indication usually is *a*.

⠆⠆ ⠆⠆   In English chord-symbol system: C minor.

⠆⠆ ⠆⠆   In English chord-symbol system: D minor.

⠆⠆ ⠆⠆   In English chord-symbol system: E minor.

⠆⠆ ⠆⠆   In English chord-symbol system: F minor.

⠆⠆ ⠆⠆   In English chord-symbol system: G minor.

⠆⠆ ⠆⠆   In English chord-symbol system: A augmented.

⠆⠆ ⠆⠆   In English chord-symbol system: B augmented.

⠆⠆ ⠆⠆   In English chord-symbol system: C augmented.

⠆⠆ ⠆⠆   In English chord-symbol system: D augmented.

⠆⠆ ⠆⠆   In English chord-symbol system: E augmented.

⠆⠆ ⠆⠆   In English chord-symbol system: F augmented.

⠆⠆ ⠆⠆   In English chord-symbol system: G augmented.

In braille edition pages 135 and 136

⠶ ⠶ In English chord-symbol system: A diminished.

⠶ ⠶ 1. Quarter-tone flat.
2. In English chord-symbol system: B diminished.

⠶ ⠶ ⠶ 1. Preceding a note: 256th note.
2. Preceding a rest: 256th rest.

⠶ ⠶ 1. Quarter-tone sharp.
2. In English chord-symbol system: C diminished.

⠶ ⠶ In English chord-symbol system: D diminished.

⠶ ⠶ In English chord-symbol system: E diminished.

⠶ ⠶ In English chord-symbol system: F diminished.

⠶ ⠶ In English chord-symbol system: G diminished.

⠶ ⠶ 1. Beginning of a square bracket above the staff.
2. In pre-1929 transcriptions: beginning of a *decrescendo* indicated by converging lines.

⠶ ⠶ 1. Literary prefix; in vocal music this marginal sign precedes a line or section of words rather than music. In literary text it indicates a return to literary characters following a music sign.

⠆⠰ ⠆⠰

2. Coincidence of notes: precedes notes that occur simultaneously in two or more parts during complex music, a *cadenza,* or an unmeasured passage. See also ⠆⠰ ⠆⠰ , definition 3, page 25.

⠆⠰ ⠆⠰   In the note-for-note method 2 only: long (extended) inverted (upper) mordent.

⠆⠰ ⠆⠰ ⠆⠰   In the note-for-note method 2 only: long (extended) mordent (lower mordent).

⠆⠰ ⠆⠰   1. The following notes or intervals are printed in normal or larger size type; may be doubled by repeating only the second half of the sign. See definition 2.

2. In Italian press braille: may indicate that the following note is in parentheses; the sign is doubled if several notes are within parentheses. See definition 1 and determine meaning from context. This meaning is usually accompanied by a transcriber's note.

⠆⠰ ⠆⠰   Ornament; long (extended) inverted (upper) mordent; precedes the note or interval it affects, and fingering, if given, follows that note or interval.

⠆⠰ ⠆⠰ ⠆⠰   Ornament; long (extended) inverted (upper) mordent that ends with an inverted turn.

110

⠒⠢ ⠢⠒ ⠒⠢   Ornament; long (extended) mordent (lower mordent); precedes the note or interval it affects. Fingering, if given, follows that note or interval.

⠢⠒ ⠢⠒ ⠒⠢ ⠢⠒   Ornament; long (extended) mordent (lower mordent) that ends with a turn.

⠒⠢ ⠢⠒ ⠒⠢ ⠢⠒ ⠒⠢   Ornament; long (extended) mordent (lower mordent) that ends with an inverted turn.

⠒⠢ ⠢⠒ ⠢⠒   Ornament; long (extended) inverted (upper) mordent that ends with a turn.

⠒⠢ ⠢⠒ ⠢⠒ ⠒⠢   Ornament; long (extended) inverted (upper) mordent that ends with an inverted turn.

⠒⠢ ⠢⠒ ⠒⠒   Ornament; long (extended) inverted (upper) mordent that ends with a turn.

⠒⠢ ⠢⠒ ⠒⠒ ⠢⠒   Ornament; long (extended) inverted (upper) mordent followed by a curve (slide) between two adjacent notes.

⠒⠢ ⠢⠒   1. Accent that is represented in print by a thick, inverted or normal *V* above or below a note; affects the following note. If written twice in succession, it is doubled for a series of nuances.

⠆⠆

2. In music for Japanese instruments: special plectrum sign that affects the following note. For koto the sign means *keshizume*, for samisen the sign means *bachikeshi*.

⠆⠆ In the note-for-note method only: ornament; a turn between the next two notes.

⠆⠆ 1. When preceded by a space: braille repeat beginning in sixth octave. The following upper or lower-cell number indicates which measure or group of measures is repeated.

2. In Rodenberg system of harmonic analysis: roman numeral. If the number that follows is in upper-cell position, it represents a capital roman numeral. Example: ⠆⠆⠆ is the IV chord. If the number that follows is in lower-cell position, it represents a small roman numeral for a minor chord. Example: ⠆⠆⠆ is the ii chord.

⠆⠆ 1. Designation for the figured bass part.

2. Marginal indication for the sixth highest voice of an ensemble.

3. In some Italian press braille transcriptions: end of a section to be repeated; in print a double bar preceded by dots. If it has this meaning, it will be followed by a space.

⠆⠆ Beginning of a square bracket shown below the staff in print.

In braille edition pages 140 and 141

⠦⠆⠴ Beginning of a square bracket below the staff that was indicated in print with a broken line; generally used to differentiate between two sets of square brackets that may overlap.

⠦⠣ In note-for-note method 2 only: accent that is represented in print by a thick *V*, either right side up or inverted.

⠦⠒⠩ In Rodenberg system of harmonic analysis: augmented chord expressed as a roman numeral. The number that follows this sign represents a roman numeral, and the dot 4 indicates the augmented chord. See ⠦⠩ , definition 2, page 112.

⠦⠆⠪ Continuation of a phrasing slur from a previous paragraph or section of music.

⠴ 1. Seventh octave; affects the note, interval, repeat, or parallel motion sign that follows. The seventh octave begins on the C three octaves above middle C, and it goes up through the next B above. If a note or repeat is preceded by two different octave signs, use the second sign for performance. See 8va, ⠬ , definition 1, page 105.

2. Replaces a comma after a musical term in literary text.

3. In the text of vocal music: the following syllable is mute.

⠆⠄

4. In Spanner system of harmonic analysis: double capital sign. If a single capital sign appears before a roman numeral that has two or more characters, it has the effect of a double capital sign.

5. In Rodenberg system of figured bass: passing note in the bass; precedes the passing note.

6. In chant notation: pointing symbol in the text; represents a short vertical bar line in print and indicates a change to the next note of the music. Dot 6 appears between spaces except in music transcribed in England, where dot 6 is not the prefix for a capital letter. In English transcriptions, dot 6 is preceded by a space and followed immediately by the first word that should be sung on the next note after the bar line.

7. Between two interval signs: moving note; indicates that a single voice of a chord moves while the remainder of the chord is sustained. This single voice is represented by interval signs on either side of the dot 6; notes so represented have equal time value unless one of the intervals is dotted (dot 3 in the next cell). In the following example a chord has two moving-note signs indicating that two single voices of the chord move while three voices are sustained. The first line shows the chord with moving notes; the second line shows the same chord written with in-accords. Read intervals up.

Example:

In braille edition pages 142-144

In the next example the moving voice has three notes. In the second line it is written with in-accords. Read intervals up.

Example: ⠒⠂ ⠶⠂ ⠢⠂ ⠔⠂ ⠢⠂ ⠶⠂ ⠒⠂ ⠔⠂
⠒⠂ ⠶⠂ ⠢⠂ ⠔⠂ ⠢⠂ ⠶⠂ ⠢⠂ ⠔⠂ ⠢⠂ ⠶⠂ ⠒⠂ ⠔⠂ ⠢⠂

In choral music a dot 6 usually implies that the moving notes are slurred. Moving notes are generally found in vertical score format.

⠢⠆ 1. In keyboard music with alternative fingerings: omission of the first fingering followed by first finger as the second fingering indication.

2. In string music: end of a line of continuation for the first finger.

⠢⠆ 1. In keyboard music with alternative fingerings: omission of the first fingering followed by second finger as the second fingering indication.

2. In string music: end of a line of continuation for the second finger.

⠒⠒ 1. Ornament; in print an inverted V between two notes (*Nachschlag*). See definition 2.

2. Slur; one method of notation indicating that two slurs meet on the same note. See definition 1 and determine meaning from context.

In braille edition pages 144 and 145   115

⠿ (braille)

⠿ **Half phrase;** in print a slur bent into an angle without actually being broken.

⠿ **Ornament;** passing note; double *appoggiatura* or slide indicated by a short curve between two adjacent notes.

⠿ 1. In keyboard music with alternative fingerings: omission of the first fingering followed by fifth finger as the second fingering indication.

2. In vocal music: square whole note whose length depends on the vocal recitative.

3. In organ pedal part: cross foot behind.

4. In music for Japanese instruments: *tsuki-iro* for koto; *suriage* and *surisage* for samisen (press and loosen string).

⠿ In keyboard music with alternative fingerings: omission of the first fingering followed by third finger as the second fingering indication.

2. In string music: end of a line of continuation for the third finger.

⠿ 1. Preceding a note: natural sign that in print was either in parentheses or above (beneath) the note.

2. Preceding an ornament: natural sign applying to the lower note of the ornament.

⠿ **Pedal release** should occur immediately after the following note or chord is played.

116   *In braille edition pages 145 and 146*

⠠⠐ 1. Preceding a note: flat sign that in print was either in parentheses or above (beneath) the note.

2. Preceding an ornament: flat sign applying to the lower note of the ornament.

⠨⠐⠨ Pedal should be depressed immediately after the next chord or note is played.

⠨⠐⠨ Distinction of rhythmic values (smaller); the following note or notes will be 16th, 32nd, 64th, or 128th notes. Applies to rests as well as notes.

⠨⠨ 1. Preceding a note: sharp sign that in print was either in parentheses or above (beneath) the note.

2. Preceding an ornament: sharp sign applying to the lower note of the ornament.

⠨⠐ 1. In keyboard music with alternative fingerings: omission of the first fingering followed by fourth finger for the second fingering indication.

2. In string music: end of a line of continuation for the fourth finger.

⠨⠐ 1. End of a square bracket placed below the staff in print.

2. In pre-1929 transcriptions: triplet within a triplet.

In braille edition pages 146 and 147   117

⠒⠂ ⠒⠢

⠒⠂ ⠒⠢   Ornament; turn above or below the following note or interval. Fingering for the turn, if given, will follow that note or interval.

⠒⠂ ⠒⠢ ⠒⠆   Ornament; inverted turn above or below the following note or interval. Fingering, if given, will follow that note or interval.

⠒⠂ ⠒⠢ ⠒⠆   Ornament; the print shows a downward curve preceding a turn.

⠒⠂ ⠒⠢   1. The following music is printed in small type; the doubled form of this sign is   ⠒⠂ ⠒⠢ ⠒⠂ .
2. In pre-1929 transcriptions: short grace note.

⠒⠂ ⠒⠢   1. The following note is *staccatissimo;* if written twice in succession, the sign is doubled.
2. In music for Japanese instruments: *utsu* for samisen and *uchizume* for koto (tap the string with a finger); applies to the following note.
3. In chant notation: words beginning with this sign and ending with   ⠒⠆ ⠒⠂   are to be sung to one note, generally the reciting note.

⠒⠂ ⠒⠢   1. Full breath.
2. In chant notation: pause.
3. In note-for-note method 2 only: long grace note; *appoggiatura.*

118   *In braille edition pages 147 and 148*

⠸⠂ ⠸⠆ 1. When preceded by a space: braille repeat beginning in seventh octave. The following upper- or lower-cell number indicates which measure or group of measures is repeated.

2. In guitar music: the number following is a fret or position sign. Example: ⠠⠂ ⠠⠆ ⠠⠂ indicates fifth fret or fifth position.

⠸⠂ ⠸⠆ Designation for the accordion part.

⠸⠂ ⠸⠆ ⠸⠂ Continuous *arpeggio* through both staves; found in older transcriptions.

⠸⠂ ⠸⠆ ⠸⠆ In string music: the next note is to be played in the seventh position or at the seventh fret. In some transcriptions the dot 6 in the first cell is part of the sign itself; in other transcriptions the dot 6 indicates a line of continuation. If a line of continuation is intended, the end of the line occurs at another position sign or when the sign ⠨⠂ ⠸⠆ appears. If the latter sign appears in any part of the transcription, then the dot 6 in the first cell of this sign indicates a line of continuation.

⠸⠂ ⠸⠆ ⠸⠂ 1. In string music: second position or second fret. Dot 6 in the first cell may indicate a line of continuation. See ⠸⠂ ⠸⠆ ⠸⠆ , above.

2. In organ music: indication for second manual.

In braille edition pages 148-150

⠠⠠⠼

⠠⠠⠼   1. In string music: third position or third fret.
Dot 6 in the first cell may indicate a line of continuation.
See ⠠⠠⠼ , page 119.

 2. In organ music: indication for third manual.

⠠⠠⠼   1. In string music: fourth position or fourth fret.
Dot 6 in the first cell may indicate a line of continuation.
See ⠠⠠⠼ , page 119.

 2. In organ music: indication for fourth manual.

⠠⠠⠼   1. In string music: first position or first fret. Dot
6 in the first cell may indicate a line of continuation.
See ⠠⠠⠼ , page 119.

 2. In organ music: indication for first manual.

⠠⠠   1. Music prefix; used before a music sign or a line of
music to distinguish it from literary text.

 2. Music parentheses; the beginning or end of parentheses
surrounding one or more music signs.

 3. In chant notation with organ accompaniment: identifies
a line that contains words alternating with melody; the line
directly below contains the remaining organ part.

 4. In Canadian melody-chord system: prefix for the
melody.

 5. In bar-by-bar format: a hyphen between parts of a
measure; i.e., right hand, left hand, and pedal parts; found
primarily in Czechoslovakian transcriptions.

⠄⠆⠒⠒ 1. Prefix for chord symbols; the following note represents the note name of a chord; the value of that note indicates its duration. If no other sign follows the note name, the chord is major; if another sign follows immediately, see the listing for that sign in the dictionary.

2. Separation between voices or parts (rare).

3. In note-for-note method 2 only: *staccatissimo*.

⠆⠒⠒ In organ pedal part: change of feet without an indication of toe or heel.

⠆⠒⠶ Ornament; long (extended) inverted (upper) mordent beginning with an inverted turn.

⠆⠒ 1. Above the seventh octave; affects the note, interval, repeat, or parallel motion sign that follows immediately. Notes above the seventh octave begin with the highest C on the piano keyboard.

2. Marginal indication for an incomplete measure or run-over line.

⠆⠒⠶ End of a square bracket below the staff indicated in print with a broken line.

FORMATS FOR BRAILLE MUSIC

A format is a general plan of organization and arrangement, and braille music has been organized and arranged in many different ways. This section identifies many of these braille music formats, sets forth their most common characteristics, and provides keys for recognition and understanding. Some of these formats are obsolete; their inclusion here does not mean they are used for transcription, merely that music in these formats is still available for use.

Since the names of formats have varied from country to country and from decade to decade, descriptions are provided. Except for chant notation, which is discussed separately, the formats in this section are gathered from braille music, transcription manuals, and catalogs and are arranged in three descriptive categories: music in parallels, music in paragraphs, and music distinguished by marginal signs.

1. This illustration contains two *parallels* of music.

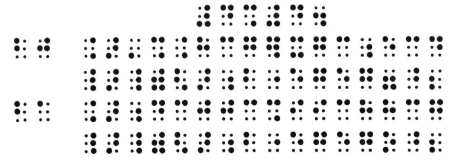

In braille edition pages 153 and 154

A parallel is a set of lines, each with music for an individual part. All of the parts contain music for the same measure(s) of the composition. A parallel may range from two lines for piano music to twenty or more lines for an orchestral score. First lines of parallels are usually preceded by measure numbers in the margins. Hand or part signs identify each line of the parallel. There may or may not be a free line between parallels.

2. This illustration contains two *paragraphs*.

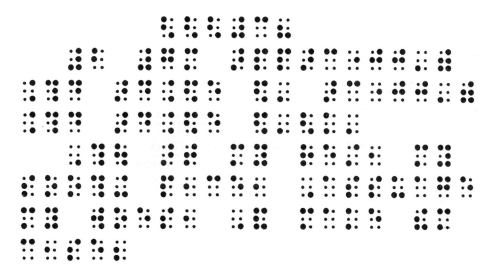

The main characteristic of a paragraph, whether music or literary braille, is that the first of a group of lines is indented. In the excerpt the first paragraph is melody and the second is corresponding text.

3. The next illustration contains eight measures of music *distinguished by marginal signs*.

In a few formats, the first line of music begins at the margin and subsequent lines begin in cell three. The left hand marginal space contains hand signs, part signs, numbers, or rehearsal letters that serve to identify new parts or locate new sections. These are the major descriptive characteristics common to music distinguished by marginal signs.

The following format identification chart is for the reader who has music in hand with no format specified on the title page. By starting with the type of music—keyboard, instrumental, vocal, or theory examples—and then examining the entries under each descriptive category— parallels, paragraphs, or marginal signs, a particular format can be identified and the explanation can be located. Since details of formats vary, only the most common characteristics are listed. The terms section-by-section and open score are found in two descriptive categories because these format titles vary between authors.

124

Format Identification Chart

I. Keyboard music
   A. Music in parallels
      1. Measures vertically aligned: bar-over-bar, page 128
      2. Measures not vertically aligned: line-over-line, page 130
      3. Many lower-cell characters and few, if any, interval signs: note-for-note, page 131
   B. Music in paragraphs
      1. Different hand signs at the beginning of the first two paragraphs; hand or pedal signs at the beginning of subsequent paragraphs: section-by-section, page 138
      2. Both hand signs usually in first paragraph; very few, if any, hand signs in subsequent paragraphs; the sign ⠶ common in the transcription: bar-by-bar, page 135
      3. Few hand signs; four-note chords notated with interval, in-accord, or moving-note signs: vertical score, page 141
      4. Many lower-cell characters and few, if any, interval signs: note-for-note, page 131
   C. Music distinguished by hand and pedal signs in margin, each followed by several lines of music: section-by-section, page 143

II. Instrumental music; solo or single part

    A. Music in paragraphs: section-by-section, page 138

    B. Music distinguished by numbers or letters in margin with run-over lines beginning in cell three: single-line, page 144

III. Instrumental music; two or more parts (score)

    A. Music in parallels

        1. Measures vertically aligned: bar-over-bar, page 128

        2. Measures not vertically aligned: line-over-line, page 130

    B. Music in paragraphs

        1. Part signs at the beginning of paragraphs: section-by-section, page 138

        2. Part signs only in the first paragraph; the sign ⠒⠒ common in the transcription: bar-by-bar, page 135

    C. Music distinguished by part signs in margin: section-by-section, page 143

IV. Vocal music; solo or single part

    A. Music in parallels; one or two text lines alternate with a line of music that begins in cell three: line-by-line, page 130

    B. Music in paragraphs

        1. Text and music in separate paragraphs: section-by-section, page 138

In braille edition pages 158 and 159

2. Text and music alternate within each paragraph: sight method, page 140

C. Music distinguished by music and literary prefixes in margin: section-by-section, page 143

V. Vocal music; two or more parts (score)

A. Music in parallels

1. Separate lines for each voice part: bar-over-bar, page 128

2. Two-line parallel with intervals and in-accord signs: short score, page 134

B. Music in paragraphs

1. Separate paragraphs for each voice part: section-by-section, page 138

2. Four-note chords notated with interval, in-accord, or moving-note signs: vertical score, page 141

3. Many lower-cell characters and few, if any, interval signs: note-for-note method, page 131

C. Music distinguished by marginal signs: section-by-section, page 143

VI. Theory and harmony examples

A. Music in parallels

1. Part signs identify each line: bar-over-bar, page 128 (Figured bass, page 155)

2. Individual notes in parallels: open score, page 133 (Figured bass, page 155)

B. Music in paragraphs: section-by-section, page 138

Music in Parallels

In the following group of formats, the initial identifying characteristic is that the braille is arranged in parallels.

Bar-over-bar. The major distinguishing characteristic of keyboard, instrumental, and vocal music in bar-over-bar format is that all lines within a parallel are aligned vertically at the beginning of measures.

Keyboard music is usually a two-line parallel (right and left hand parts) with a third line added when there is an organ pedal part. An unidentified line indented two cells is a run-over containing music for the part on the line above. Additional lines identified with hand signs may appear in a parallel for contrapuntal or highly complex music. This practice is sometimes called open score format, but since the need for extra lines is usually temporary, the term "open score" rarely appears on the title page.

Since bar-over-bar is one of the oldest formats and has been used throughout the world, there are many variations. Some music has octave signs at the beginning of each measure and some does not; some measure numbers have numeral prefixes but most do not. Occasionally in early transcriptions when run-over lines were not used, a hand sign will be followed by no music at all. The part with music is the end of a measure; the part without music was completed in the parallel above.

If the right hand part begins with a dynamic marking applicable to both parts, the left hand part is sometimes

In braille edition pages 160 and 161

indented so that the music itself is vertically aligned. This practice is not consistent, and a dynamic marking in the right hand part is generally understood to apply to all parts.

Chords and intervals in pedal and left hand parts should be read up. Right hand parts often read down; but a large body of music in bar-over-bar format, especially that transcribed between 1930 and 1956, has the right hand keyboard parts reading up. When there is no transcribers's note giving the direction of intervals, examine the in-accords, which are usually written the same direction as the intervals. If the notes before the in-accord sign are higher than those coming after that sign, the intervals of that part should read down; if the notes before the in-accord are lower, the intervals should read up. Fingering may also give clues to direction; a note played with the thumb of the right hand will be the bottom note of a chord, while a note played by the fifth finger of that hand will be the top note.

Instrumental scores contain one line for each part, with measure alignment and other characteristics of music in parallels. Expression marks, and any other information centered above a parallel, apply to all parts. Intervals read up in lower-range instruments such as the cello and string bass and down in treble instruments such as the violin and viola.

Choral scores contain one or more lines of text, depending on whether all parts sing the same words. Music lines, usually one line for each voice part, are placed in a parallel either above or below the words. For the correlation of words with music, see page 179. Intervals read up in men's parts and down in women's parts.

Line-by-line. This format is used either for solo vocal music or for individual choral parts. A line of text alternates with a line of music for the words above, giving the general appearance of a parallel, and each of the lines within that parallel contains text or music for the same measures of the composition. While the text line or the music line may run over onto a second line, both parts will rarely run over at the same time. When a text line runs over, it is indented to cell five, since music lines always begin in cell three.

Occasionally two lines of text appear at the margin, followed by the music line as the third line of the parallel. This practice occurs when the text is given in two languages, and also when two verses are given for the same music. If there are more than two verses of text, the first one is given above the music, and the remaining verses are written at the end of the piece. For the correlation of text with melody, see page 179 and definitions of individual music signs.

When chord symbols are used in line-by-line format, they are written on a separate line, or they are placed in the melody line preceded by the prefix ⠒⠒ . See chord symbols, page 148.

Line-over-line. This format is a variation of bar-over-bar and is used primarily for keyboard music. Except for the distinguishing characteristic that measures within a parallel are not aligned vertically, the only other difference is that a greater freedom is allowed in the use of run-over lines; one

In braille edition pages 163 and 164

part may have several run-over lines within a parallel. For an explanation of run-over lines and a general description of the format, see bar-over-bar, page 128. Line-over-line is sometimes listed as a vocal music format. In this section that format is described under the heading line-by-line, page 130.

Note-for-note. The music appears at first reading to contain an unusual number of staccato notes, grace notes, turns, and trills. In place of interval signs, lower-cell characters appear in the music.

The term "note-for-note" refers to the way in which chords are written. Instead of interval signs to designate the members of a chord, subnotes (note names written in the lower-cell position) are used.

Example: (read up) ⠽ ⠖ ⠦ ⠣ ⠴

This is the chord, C E G B-flat. The notes E, G, and B are formed as note names written in the lower part of the cell. The first note of the chord is written normally with its rhythmic value indication, and the flat sign is also unchanged. The accidental precedes the subnote as in other formats, and fingering, if given, follows a subnote. The upward or downward direction of reading chords follows general practice (up for left hand and lower-range instruments; usually down for right hand and higher instrumental parts). Octave signs are used when necessary to indicate a unison or an interval greater than an octave between two subnotes or between a normal note and a subnote.

Example: (read up) ⠘ ⠽ ⠸ ⠖

The above example is second octave C played with third octave E forming a tenth. Doubling of subnotes is not allowed except for the doubling of octaves.

The braille characters used in forming subnotes have other, more common meanings. The subnote G, for example, is a sign that also means staccato. In some note-for-note music both sets of meanings are used, and in other music only one meaning is possible for each lower-cell sign. If Method 1 is designated on the title page, both sets of meanings are used. In this music a hyphen (dots 3-6) is placed before a symbol if it should not be read as a subnote; the hyphen is used only where there might be confusion. When the hyphen is not necessary, as in the beginning of the following example, it is not included.

Example: (read down)

The first sign cannot be a subnote since it does not follow a normal note; it is a staccato sign that is doubled. The next time that sign appears, it is the subnote G. Near the end of the measure it is to be read as a staccato sign rather than a subnote, so it is preceded by the hyphen. The next example is the same measure written with interval signs (not note-for-note) for comparison.

Example: (read down)

In braille edition pages 166 and 167

If Method 2 is designated on the title page, note names in the lower-cell position are always subnotes. Signs that indicate intervals in other formats have been given the meanings of trill, grace note, staccato, etc. in this format. These meanings are included in the dictionary.

The sign ⠒⠒ (dots 3-6) means staccato in this method, and the following example is the same measure as above, now written in the second version of the note-for-note format.

Example: (read down)

If a composition does not carry the designation "Method 1" or "Method 2," an examination of the above material with the possible definitions listed for individual music signs should reveal which method was used in the transcription. The note-for-note method may be found in paragraphs (section-by-section, bar-by-bar, vertical score, etc.) as well as in parallels.

Open Score. This term has several meanings. Those listed below apply only to music that is written in parallels. For choral music that is written in paragraphs, see open score on page 134.

In keyboard music, open-score format means that more than one line of a parallel contains music for a single part; i.e., a parallel may have two lines of music for the right hand part. See bar-over-bar, page 128, for further explanation of the extra lines and the other characteristics of this music.

In choral music, open score means that each vocal part has a separate line of music in the parallel. The term is interchangeable with bar-over-bar (page 128).

Music theory and harmony examples are sometimes written in an open-score format. In this case, each voice is given a separate line of a parallel so that no interval signs are necessary; i.e., four-note chords are written in a four-line parallel. The music is aligned at the beginning of each measure, and sometimes the beginning of each beat is also vertically aligned. In the latter case, the sign ⠒⠂ is often used to show print bar lines. If figured bass is included with theory examples, see figured bass, page 155.

Short-form Scoring. Although sometimes listed on a title page, short-form scoring is an interior format. See page 149.

Short Score. A choral score for three or more parts is reduced to a two-line parallel. In a short score, the women's voice parts are combined in one line of a parallel and the men's voice parts are written in the other line. Intervals or in-accords are used to combine the voice parts, and these read down in the top line (women's voices) and up in the bottom line (men's voices). In music for a trio, one line, of course, has no intervals or in-accords. The beginning of each measure is vertically aligned as in bar-over-bar format, page 128.

The text for this musical score is written in a paragraph or set of paragraphs, and the accompaniment is written separately in its own format.

In braille edition pages 169 and 170

Music in Paragraphs

In the following group of formats, the initial identifying characteristic is that the braille is arranged in paragraphs. **Bar-by-bar.** The music usually has more than one hand or part sign in the opening paragraph and no hand or part signs in subsequent paragraphs. Most paragraphs have several bar line signs ⠿ each preceded and followed by a space. In bar-by-bar format a composition is divided into sections, and each complete section with all of its parts comprises a paragraph. Within a paragraph all parts of a measure, or bar, are written consecutively from the lowest to the highest with a space between each part. A bar line ⠇⠂ signals the end of a complete measure, and succeeding measures are written similarly. Thus, the music is presented "bar-by-bar."

In the first measure, each part is introduced with its appropriate hand or part sign. In the following measures these hand or part signs do not appear unless there is a change in the order or number of parts. Intervals and in-accords usually read up in all parts. The following is a two-measure example of bar-by-bar organ music.

In the second measure the left hand plays a repeated chord, and the right hand repeats measure one.

If the music is temporarily reduced to one part for several measures, the bar line sign is no longer necessary, and a space indicates the end of a measure. If all parts are silent for one or more bars, a single rest or a combination sign such as ⠆ ⠒ ⠰ is used. Repeats are treated in the same way if they affect all parts. The part-measure in-accord sign is often used as a whole-measure in-accord, since it can apply to an entire measure of one part but never to all parts of the bar.

Paragraphs are usually numbered or identified by page and line. The numbering may be consecutive throughout the composition, or it may indicate the staves on each print page. Some bar-by-bar music has a measure number at the beginning of each line. This number usually identifies the first measure to begin on that line, not necessarily the music that appears immediately after the number. If no new measure begins on the line, the marginal space is filled with dot 6s.

In the Czechoslovakian variation of this format, keyboard music has the right hand part first with intervals reading down. This is followed by the left hand and then the pedal parts with intervals reading up. All parts are connected by dots 6, 3 acting as a hyphen. Spaces occur only at the bar line or between measures when parts are combined so that a bar line is not necessary.

New Style. Around 1918 music was brailled by the National Institute for the Blind, London, with "New Style" shown on the title page. This music was written in a variation of the bar-by-bar format (page 135) with the symbols and practices

136   *In braille edition pages 172 and 173*

of what is now known as old style music (following). The substitution method of notating pitches that frequently change octaves was employed in this music. Substitution is explained with the sign ⠿⠿⠿ on page 93.

Old Style. This is a term used in catalogs of braille music, rather than a format described in any manual of braille music transcription. The term is applied to music written section-by-section in paragraphs with some of the old signs and practices of braille transcription. The most noticeable differences between the old style and modern transcription of music are the tie sign, the use of octave signs, and the use of dot 3. The sign ⠿⠿ means a tie rather than an accumulating *arpeggio;* octave signs are used according to the original rules (page 167) and are not repeated after an in-accord sign or at the beginning of a new line unless necessary according to those rules; dot 3 is not used as a separation between a literary abbreviation and the music symbol that follows. Another difference is the pre-1929 method of writing alternating or reiterated chords and notes, but the majority of music signs have the same meaning in both old style and modern transcription.

Open Score. This term as applied to choral music written in paragraphs means that the music for each voice part is written in separate paragraphs rather than being combined in a short score (page 134) or a vertical score (page 141). The composition is usually divided into sections unless the song is very short. The text for the first section is written in a paragraph with any variations of words between different voice parts noted. The music for this portion of the text is written in separate paragraphs for each voice part, and these paragraphs are labelled. Succeeding paragraphs retain the order of paragraphs established in the first section. For the correlation of text with melody, see page 179.

If the term "open score" is applied to music written in parallels, see page 133.

Paragraph Format. Consult section-by-section (following) for a description of music listed in some catalogs as written in paragraph format. In this dictionary the word paragraph is used to help identify a group of formats.

Phrase Method. Consult section-by-section, which follows.

Section-by-section. The major identifying characteristic of keyboard, vocal, or instrumental music in section-by-section format is that each paragraph is identified with a hand or part sign. For section-by-section music that is not written in paragraphs, see page 143.

In section-by-section format a composition is divided into sections by its musical phrasing, by the staves on the print page, or by some other plan. The music for the first section is written with a separate paragraph for each part (right hand, left hand; soprano, alto, bass; violin, viola, cello, etc.). When the music for the first section has been completed for all parts, the music for the second section begins with the parts presented in the same order. From the second section on, the first paragraph of each section usually begins with a rehearsal letter or a number. The number may be consecutive throughout the composition, or it may represent the staves on each print page.

Every paragraph within the section begins with a hand or part sign, except for a solo instrumental or vocal part consisting of only one paragraph for each section of music. The piano accompaniment for an instrumental or vocal solo will have three paragraphs for each section—solo line, right hand, and left hand—each identified with its hand or part sign.

In keyboard music, hand signs within a paragraph may indicate notes to be played by the left hand in the right hand paragraph of music and vice versa, but most paragraphs contain only the initial hand sign. Intervals and chords read up in pedal and left hand parts; down in right hand parts. Dynamics in the right hand part generally apply to all parts.

In instrumental music intervals read up for lower-range instruments and down for treble instruments.

In vocal music the text appears in a paragraph or set of paragraphs separate from the music. In some compositions the text precedes the music and in some compositions it follows, but since music can rarely be read as a word or vice versa, the plan for any given composition is easily determined. In choral music each voice part is given a separate paragraph. If intervals are used, such as in a part that is temporarily divided, the intervals read up for men's voices and down for women's voices. The text will only be written once if all parts sing the same words. For correlation of words with melody, see page 179.

In braille edition pages 174-176

Sight Method. This format for vocal music was devised as a means of putting text and melody as close together as possible. A single syllable, word, or very short group of words alternate with one or more notes within each paragraph. A space indicates a change from literary to music braille and vice versa. Since some uncapitalized words can appear to be music, they are usually preceded by a hyphen; hyphens also link groups of words in order to avoid leaving a space between them. Notes are not preceded by octave signs unless necessary according to the original rules (page 167). One note is sung with each syllable of text unless slurs link the notes or hyphens separate them. The following excerpt from a folk song is in four-four time.

Example:

The text is "Sweeter far than dreaming." There is one note per syllable until the last word. The slur indicates that the first syllable of "dreaming" is sung to the eighth notes A and F-sharp. The final character is the sign for a bar line.

When the sight method is used for chant music, a hyphen in the music indicates a change of syllable in the text.

Example:

In braille edition pages 177-179

In the example above, the text is "Alleluia, Deo." Symbols of chant notation in the music portion include the *ictus* ⠶⠶ , ⠶ which doubles the value of the note D, and a breath mark ⠶ .

In the following example, each word is divided into syllables, and each syllable is followed immediately by its note.

Example:

⠶⠶⠶ ⠶⠶ ⠶⠶⠶⠶ ⠶⠶⠶ ⠶⠶⠶ ⠶
⠶⠶⠶ ⠶⠶⠶

The text is "Et Angelus." As can be seen from the examples, there are variations in this format, but the major characteristic, the alternation of words and music on the same line, is retained.

Stave-by-stave. In this music the length of the print staves determines the length of the paragraphs. Other details are the same as section-by-section, page 138.

Vertical Score. This format is used more frequently for hymns and chorales than for any other type of music. Whether written for chorus, piano, or organ, the music generally has four-note chords throughout. In choral music, the four parts are combined and written as chords. In most cases the bass note is followed by interval signs representing the voices above, and chords read up. An interval reads down only if it is preceded by dot 4. In keyboard music, the parts for pedal, left hand, and right hand are combined and written in chords usually beginning with the bass note and reading up. In the first measure, pedal and hand signs may indicate which notes are played in which part, but these signs are not always included. A dot 4 in the middle of a chord indicates that the intervals following it should be played by the right hand.

In both choral and keyboard music, the sign ⠿ indicates a unison of voices. In-accords are used to indicate moving voices in some music, and in other compositions these are replaced by the sign ⠡ before an interval to indicate one moving note, or ⠩ before an interval to indicate two or more moving notes. See ⠻ , definition 7, page 114 for an explanation of moving notes.

The following short segment in four-four time is for SATB chorus. The paragraph begins with an identification of the print page, line, and bar numbers. In each chord the first note is the bass part, the first interval sign is the tenor part, the second interval sign is the alto part, and the final note of the chord is the soprano part.

Example:

The text for the choral music parts above is written in paragraphs identified with page, line, and bar numbers.

In braille edition pages 180 and 181

Music Distinguished by Marginal Signs

In the following group of formats, the initial identifying characteristics are hand signs, part signs, measure numbers, or rehearsal letters that appear in the margin, followed by several indented lines.

Continental Style. Consult section-by-section format that follows.

Section-by-section. In keyboard, vocal, or instrumental music, hand or part signs are prominent in the left margin. For solo music with measure numbers or rehearsal letters outstanding in the left margin, consult single-line, page 144. For section-by-section music written in paragraphs, see page 138.

Section-by-section music is divided according to musical phrases, staves on the print page, rehearsal letters, or some other plan. Beginning with the second section, a centered heading on a free line usually identifies new sections. This heading gives the serial number of the section (upper-cell number), inclusive measure numbers of the section (lower-cell numbers), print page numbers, and sometimes staff numbers. Within a section each part begins at the margin with its hand or part sign and continues on lines that begin in cell three. Intervals in left hand parts, pedal parts, men's voice parts, and parts for lower-range instruments read up. Intervals in other parts generally read down.

In vocal music the literary prefix (dots 5-6, 2-3) is the marginal sign for each section of the text. This section is followed by the music with its prefix (dots 6, 3) in the margin. In some vocal music labelled section-by-section, just one line of words is followed by one line of music, each line beginning at the margin. In this case the sections are not labelled on a free line. Other vocal music is in longer sections, with the characteristic run-over lines beginning in cell three. For the correlation of words with music, see page 179.

Single-line. This format is used for a single instrumental part of an ensemble or for an instrumental solo. The music is presented in segments, usually two to five lines in length. The initial line of each segment begins at the margin with a measure number, rehearsal number, or rehearsal letter; the run-over lines begin in cell three. If rehearsal letters are being used, the first line begins in cell three instead of cell one; subsequent segments begin in cell one with a rehearsal letter.

Intervals and in-accords read up for lower-range instruments such as cello and bassoon; the intervals and in-accords generally read down for treble instruments such as viola and trumpet.

Solo Style. Consult single-line format above.

Chant Notation

Chant notation refers to sacred vocal music known as chants, canticles, plainsong, psalm tones, etc. Some of these are written entirely in modern notation, a few have been

144

In braille edition pages 183 and 184

transcribed from square notes or neumatic print notation, and most have standard notes and rhythmic values combined with features retained from the older notation such as reciting notes, breath signs, and no time signature. Formats for chant notation are discussed in the final paragraph of this section.

Square notes or neumes are written as specific pitches in braille, although the singer is free to transpose and sing within his voice range. Eighth notes represent the basic rhythmic unit. This unit is never divided, and if it is to be lengthened, an additional sign (such as dot 1, which means to double the note) appears in braille. In neumatic notation, dots 3 and 6 in the same cell as a note name do not indicate rhythmic value. Instead, dot 3 indicates that a pitch is the first note of a neume, dot 6 identifies a liquescent note, and dots 3-6 indicate a *quilisma*. It can be determined by context whether the above meanings apply or whether dots 3 and 6 are rhythmic value indications. A rest sign indicates the modern notation of rhythm with quarter, half, and whole notes, since breath or bar line signs are used in place of rests in neumatic notation.

It is advisable to check the dictionary for meanings related to chant notation. Definitions of signs for square-note music begin with the phrase, "in neumatic notation"; definitions that apply either to square or round notation begin with the phrase, "in chant notation."

Many forms of chant music have no time signature. In this case, a space in the braille music line often indicates the end of a word rather than the end of a measure. The correlation of words with melody may follow modern practice using slurs (page 179) or it may depend on hyphens (dots 3-6). A hyphen in the braille music line indicates a change of syllable in the text. Notes not separated by either a hyphen or a space are sung to one syllable. The text may also be hyphenated to show syllabic divisions of words.

Example:

In the above example the first syllable of "Deum" is sung on three notes. Each space in the music line indicates the end of a word, not the end of a measure. This example illustrates chant music that is a combination of round notation and special symbols for chant music. The eighth note (which is used as the basic rhythmic unit for chant notation) appears in this example along with hyphens in the music line. Spacing is at the end of each word. The eighth rest, however, indicates round notes in print, so dot 6 in the braille character just before the eighth rest shows that the note E is a quarter note, not a liquescent note.

Chant texts may be pointed for correlation with the notes of the ecclesiastical modes. In this case, the braille contains special signs including some that may appear to be punctuation. For example: a dot 6 in the text may appear to be a capital sign, but it may instead represent a print sign meaning to change notes in the chant music; a colon refers to

In braille edition pages 185-187

a double bar line in the music; and quotation marks surround a syllable that should be sung on two notes (rather than the modern use of quotation marks putting two syllables on one note).

Chant music is written in several formats. The sight method (page 140) is used for older transcriptions. The illustration on page 140 is transcribed from neumatic notation. The section-by-section format (page 138) has text (with or without pointing) in paragraphs separate from the music. In the line-by-line format (page 130), each line of text is followed by an indented line of music.

INTERIOR FORMATS

Chord symbols, figured bass, and harmonic analysis are areas which require special formats that are integrated into overall formats. There is more than one special format for each of these areas. For instance, the Spanner short-form scoring system for chord symbols is different from the English system for chord symbols. Moreover, Spanner symbols may be found in music written either in parallels or in paragraphs.

Chord Symbols

In print chord symbols, G represents a G major chord, Gm represents a G minor chord, and G7 represents a G seventh chord. At least four distinct systems have been developed for the braille notation of such symbols. The system described in Spanner's *Revised International Manual of Braille Music Notation 1956* is referred to as Spanner short-form scoring in this dictionary. The Canadian melody-chord system was developed by the National Music Transcription Bureau of the Canadian National Institute for the Blind (CNIB). The English system is used especially for popular music by the Royal National Institute for the Blind, London. The fourth system, a literal presentation of letters and numbers instead of special braille characters, was introduced in the Spanner

In braille edition pages 188 and 189

manual and developed further in the United States.

In print a diagram sometimes accompanies a chord symbol to show the position of the fingers on the strings and frets of a plucked instrument. In this dictionary such a diagram is referred to as tablature.

Spanner Short-form Scoring. This system uses a set of special signs to represent chord symbols. These signs appear with the words and melody of a song and are usually found in the melody line following the short-form scoring prefix ⠠⠶ (dots 6, 3-6). Occasionally the signs are found on a free line below the music with no prefix. The chord symbols consist of a note name with rhythmic indication plus other signs or numbers as necessary. Accidentals always precede the note or number they modify.

Example:

In the example above the first measure of music has three quarter notes followed by the short-form scoring prefix and two chord symbols. The first chord symbol consists of the quarter note C and the suffix ⠰ that indicates minor. The quarter note indication means that this chord symbol applies only to the first beat of the measure. The second chord symbol is B-flat seventh. The half note rhythmic value shows that this symbol applies to two beats of music. The second measure has a dotted half note, a short-form prefix, and the

E-flat chord symbol for three beats. A chord symbol that does not have a suffix is a major chord. The major chord symbols and all of the suffixes are defined in the dictionary with the initial phrase, "in Spanner short-form scoring."

Canadian Melody-chord System. The Canadian National Institute for the Blind (CNIB) system of short-form scoring follows the same general principles as the Spanner system. Special chord symbols are written in the melody line following the prefix ⠠⠶ (dots 6, 3-6), chord names are formed like note names, and rhythmic value indications are used. Major chords are identical in the Canadian and Spanner systems. The difference between the two systems consists of a different set of suffixes for minor, diminished, and augmented chords, and the Canadian use of interval signs to represent the numbers of print chord symbols. Accidentals precede the note or the interval they modify.

Example:

This illustration contains the same music and chord symbols as are in the illustration of Spanner short-form scoring. In the first measure of music the short-form prefix appears after the three quarter notes and is followed by the two chord symbols. The C minor chord symbol consists of the quarter note C and the suffix ⠦ that means minor.

In braille edition pages 190-192

The rhythmic value shows that this symbol applies only to the first beat. The second chord symbol is B-flat seventh. It applies to two beats and the sign for an interval of a seventh represents the number seven. The E-flat major chord symbol for all three beats of the second measure is identical to Spanner short-form scoring.

When studying music published by CNIB, refer to the definitions in the dictionary that begin with the phrase, "in the Canadian melody-chord system."

English Chord-symbol System. In popular music published by the Royal National Institute for the Blind (RNIB), the symbol for a major chord is a literary braille letter preceded by a letter sign. For example, the G major chord sysbol is ⠰⠛ . Dot 3 added to this character represents a minor chord, dot 6 indicates a diminished chord, and dots 3-6 mean the chord is augmented. The following signs represent the G minor, G diminished, and G augmented chord symbols respectively: ⠰⠛ ⠰⠛ ⠰⠛ . Numbers are used if they appear in print, and accidentals precede the letter or number they modify. The chord symbols are found in the accompaniment part and are located on a free line above the measure to which they apply. No rhythmic value is indicated.

Example:

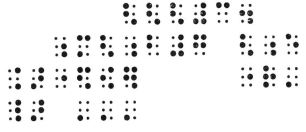

This is the same music shown in the examples of the other chord-symbol systems. The first chord is C minor. The performer determines either by ear or with his knowledge of harmony that the change to the B-flat seventh chord should occur on the second beat of the first measure. The final chord is E-flat major.

Print chord symbols are sometimes followed immediately by an oblique line and a capital letter that specifies which note should be played in the bass. In the RNIB system this is shown by following the note to be played in the bass with a *b* and a period.

Example: ⠒⠂ ⠒⠆ ⠒⠂ ⠒⠆ ⠒⠂ ⠒⠂ ⠒⠆

The example is the chord symbol for F-sharp minor with A in the bass. These and other symbols are defined in the dictionary following the phrase, "in English chord-symbol system."

Literal Chord Symbols. Letters and numbers are written in literary braille, unspaced, just as they appear in print. Music signs are used for accidentals and follow the order of the print; they are not rearranged to precede a letter. The sign ⠖ (dots 3-4-6) represents the print plus sign, and the sign ⠔ (dots 3-6) represents the hyphen or minus sign. Other characters, such as parentheses or oblique lines, are written in literary braille. In most cases the chord symbols are written on a free line between the word line and the melody line of vocal music or beneath the left hand part of keyboard music.

In braille edition pages 193-195

In a vocal part the chord symbols are aligned either with the notes of the melody or with the syllables of the words. The latter case is almost always accompanied by a transcriber's note. If aligned with the melody, the initial sign of a chord symbol is placed directly over the note or the rest where the chord change should occur.

Example:

In the example above the first line is text, the second line is chord symbols, and those symbols are aligned directly above the melody notes in the third line. Note that the melody is hyphenated where necessary in order to maintain alignment with the chord symbols.

When the chord symbols are aligned with the text, the initial sign of the chord symbol is placed directly below the first braille character of the syllable where the chord change occurs. If the change occurs during a rest, the initial sign of the chord symbol is aligned so that it falls between words, and if the change occurs during a syllable, a hyphen (dots 3-6) is placed directly below the beginning of that syllable and followed immediately by the chord symbol.

Example:

⠀⠀⠀⠀⠀⠀⠀⠀⠿⠀⠇⠀⠇⠀⠯⠀⠹⠀⠿

⠀⠀⠹⠀⠏⠀⠿⠀⠀⠹⠀⠏⠀⠀⠹⠀⠏⠀⠀⠹⠀⠿

⠀⠀⠹⠀⠿⠀⠏⠀⠀⠹⠀⠯⠀⠇⠀⠿⠀⠀⠹⠀⠏⠀⠿

⠀⠀⠀⠀⠹⠀⠿⠀⠿⠀⠀⠹⠀⠯⠀⠏⠀⠿

The melody in the example above was changed slightly from the previous illustrations so that the final chord change occurs during the word "me." The chord line is between the word line and the melody line, but the alignment is with the words above rather than the melody below. The hyphen indicates that the chord changes while "me" is sung, and, as in the RNIB system, the performer determines when that change occurs either by ear or with his knowledge of harmony.

Tablature. This term refers to the diagram showing strings, frets, and fingering that often accompanies a chord symbol. Tablature notation designating pitches and rhythmic values is not transcribed into braille. Tablature diagrams may be transcribed, however, and they are usually placed in a special note section or at the beginning of a piece.

The name of the chord symbol is written first and is followed by the signs for string, *barré,* fret, and finger in that order. After a space the next string, *barré,* fret, and finger signs are given. If a string is omitted, it is not played. *Barré* signs are used only where they apply.

154   *In braille edition pages 196 and 197*

Example:

⠿⠿ ⠿⠿⠿ ⠿⠿⠿⠿⠿ ⠿⠿⠿ ⠿⠿⠿⠿⠿
⠿⠿⠿⠿⠿

The tablature for the C major chord in the example above reads: C; first string, open; second string, first fret, first finger; third string, open; fourth string, second fret, second finger; fifth string, third fret, third finger.

In some transcriptions the strings are given in reverse order. Another variation is the use of numeral signs for the frets as well as for fingering. In all variations the order of signs remains the same: string, fret, finger.

Ukulele chords are written as above or in a shorter system that omits the string signs since all four strings are always played. Fret signs are written as lower-cell numbers without the numeral prefix. The order of signs remains the same as in the longer system.

Example: ⠿⠿ ⠿⠿⠿⠿⠿⠿

The tablature for the F major ukulele chord above reads: F; open string, first fret, first finger, open string, second fret, second finger.

Figured Bass

Two distinct systems for figured bass have been used in the United States. The older of these was outlined in the Cologne key of 1888 and developed further in Rodenberg's *Key to Braille Music Notation*, 1925. The newer system has been in use since the publication of Spanner's *Revised International Manual of Braille Music Notation 1956.*

Rodenberg System. In this method print numerals are written in braille as intervals; i.e., the sign for the interval of a sixth represents the figured bass numeral six. The interval of a second is used for the numeral nine. Numerals in a vertical column in print are written horizontally in braille in ascending order, following the bass note to which they apply. If two or more numerals appear side by side in print indicating a change of harmony on one note, the sign ⠦ (dots 2-5) comes between the corresponding interval signs.

An accidental always precedes the number it modifies, except when followed by dot 3. In this case, it stands alone in print, indicating an altered third. A dot 4 represents a print dash after a figure. The following example is one measure of figured bass in the Rodenberg system.

Example:

The above measure in four-four time is read: third octave F-sharp (eighth note) with sharp 6 under it; second octave B (eighth note); D-sharp (eighth note) with a vertical column reading from the bottom up: sharp, 5, 6; B (eighth note);

In braille edition pages 198-200

third octave E (dotted quarter note) with 4 under it changing to 3 and then changing to flat 5; G (eighth note) with isolated flat and 6 under it.

Definitions of all signs used in this system of figured bass notation are identified by the phrase "in Rodenberg system of figured bass."

Spanner System. Braille signs for figured bass described in the Spanner manual are used in two different arrangements. Sometimes they are written horizontally on the same line with the bass notes, and sometimes they are written vertically in a facsimile representation of the print arrangement of figured bass symbols. Common to both arrangements are the prefix ⠆⠆ and the use of lower-cell numerals.

In the horizontal arrangement a number sign precedes every column of numbers or figures, and the numbers are written in ascending order. If two numbers are each preceded by a number sign, they were side by side in print rather than in a column. An accidental precedes the number it modifies, but it follows a numeral sign. The hyphen (dots 3-6) precedes a lower-cell sign if that sign should be read as a turn, grace note, trill, etc., instead of a number. The sign ⠒ preceding an accidental means that the accidental stands alone in print, indicating an altered third. Definitions for these and other figures such as dashes and oblique lines are identified by the phrase, "in Spanner system of figured bass."

The following example is the same figured bass measure as above. It is written in Spanner figured bass notation with the horizontal arrangement of figures.

Example:

⠀⠀⠀⠀⠀⠀⠀⠀⠀⠀⠀⠀⠀⠀⠀⠀⠀

⠀⠀⠀⠀⠀⠀⠀⠀⠀⠀⠀⠀⠀⠀⠀⠀⠀⠀⠀⠀⠀⠀⠀⠀⠀

This illustration is read the same as the illustration for the Rodenberg system.

The vertical arrangement is not shown in the Spanner manual. In this modern adaptation of the Spanner system, the numbers and figures are aligned vertically below the notes in braille as in print. The number sign appears only at the top of each column. If a chord change occurs on a sustained note, the columns of figures are separated by hyphens. If necessary, the notes in the bass line are spaced to make room for accidentals and other signs associated with the figures below. No prefix is necessary for isolated accidentals, and modifying accidentals follow the numbers to which they apply.

The following example is the same measure of figured bass as above, written in the vertical arrangement of Spanner figured bass notation.

Example:

⠀⠀⠀⠀⠀⠀⠀⠀⠀⠀⠀⠀⠀⠀⠀⠀⠀

⠀⠀⠀⠀⠀⠀⠀⠀⠀⠀⠀⠀⠀⠀⠀⠀⠀⠀⠀⠀⠀⠀⠀⠀⠀

158

Harmonic Analysis

In the Rodenberg system of harmonic analysis, a roman numeral is a letter sign followed by a number. The number is in upper-cell position for an upper-case numeral and in the lower-cell position for a lower-case numeral. If the roman numeral is followed by one or more arabic numerals, these are shown as lower-cell numbers and are written without a numeral prefix of their own. In the following example, the harmonic progression, I ii $\mathrm{IV}_{\substack{6\\4}}$ V_7 I, is shown in this form of harmonic analysis.

Example:

The Spanner manual does not cover harmonic analysis, but the practice of writing upper-case roman numerals as double capitals and lower-case roman numerals with a letter sign is now followed. In some modern transcriptions a single capital sign is used for all upper-case roman numerals. The practice of writing arabic numerals as lower-cell numbers with no number sign has been continued; the bottom print number is given first. The following example shows the chord progression, I ii $\mathrm{IV}_{\substack{6\\4}}$ V_7 I, in the modern system of notation.

Example:

When harmonic analysis and figured bass are both shown with the same music, each has its own line(s) of braille. Harmonic analysis is usually placed beneath figured bass.

FUNDAMENTALS
OF BRAILLE MUSIC

This section is an introduction to braille notation (included for readers of the print edition) and to braille music devices. This information should be supplemented by the dictionary definitions. Additional materials are suggested in the annotated list of resources at the end.

The Braille System

Braille is a system for reading that uses raised-dot symbols. Each braille character consists of one or more dots from a full cell of six dots arranged as follows: ⠿ . The dots in each cell are numbered from top to botton, 1-2-3 on the left side of the cell and 4-5-6 on the right. Sixty-three different characters can be formed from a full cell; each is listed in the table of contents in the standard order of braille signs. The three braille codes (literary, music, and mathematical) utilize these same characters in the same order.

In the literary braille code the first twenty-five signs are the letters of the alphabet from *a* to *z* except for *w*. *W* appears later because when the code was devised it was a diphthong in the French alphabet, not a single letter. Other characters are punctuation signs, signs for contractions (groups of letters), short words, and composition signs. Composition signs are symbols indicating a change of type (capital letter, italics) or symbols giving special meaning to a character that follows (letter sign, number sign). A single braille character may have different meanings according to its use. The symbol ⠃ , for example, is "b" when part of a word, the word "but" when standing alone, and "2" when preceded by the number sign. Letter combinations may also indicate whole words (ab = about, ac = according). Complete rules for literary braille are contained in *English Braille American Edition*.

Braille Music in Brief

Braille music is not written on a staff; it is written in horizontal lines of braille characters. Most pages of music contain both literary and music notation. The literary material (*allegro, cresc., dolce*) is written in the literary code and is separated from the music by its placement or by a sign that alerts the reader to the change of code. Complete words or phrases are surrounded with literary parentheses and separated from music by at least one space. Abbreviations such as *rit.* or *dim.* are preceded by the word sign ⠲ . Another sign ⠰⠰ , generally used in textbook material, shows the return to the literary code after a musical example.

Each measure of music is separated from the next measure by a space. Pitches are designated by letter and octave rather than by location on a staff. While clef signs are sometimes included in the braille transcription, they do not affect the names of the notes.

A chord is written as a note with intervals. Only the top or the bottom note of a chord is identified by its letter name; the other members of the chord are expressed with interval signs. When it is not possible to notate the contents of a measure with chords because of differing rhythmic values between parts, the contrapuntal voices are written horizontally and are linked together with the in-accord sign ⠿ ⠿ to indicate a simultaneous performance.

Braille music contains every detail from the print page unless a transcriber's note indicates that some portion of the print was omitted from the braille copy. Accidentals, slurs, accents, dynamics, fingering, pedaling, bowing, etc., are interspersed among the notes in the horizontal lines of braille characters, and when a series of notes must receive the same marking, such as staccato, the braille sign is doubled to avoid constant repetition (it is written twice in succession at the beginning of the series and repeated once at the end of the series).

In addition to understanding the signs of braille music, a reader must also understand the format or general arrangement of the signs. Piano music, for example, is written in two parts (right hand and left hand) that correspond roughly to the treble and bass staves of print music. These two parts may be arranged in parallel lines similar to print with each measure vertically aligned, the right and left hand parts may be written in separate paragraphs of music, or the parts may be arranged in other configurations. (See formats for braille music, page 122.)

Reading vocal music in braille requires an understanding of the correlation between words and melody, since these are not aligned vertically in braille as they are in print. The words and melody are written either on alternating parallel lines or in alternating paragraphs, while the accompaniment—including an outline of the vocal melody—is written separately. Choral music has parallel lines or paragraphs for each voice part. Sometimes the text and sometimes the melody is given first, but since it is extremely rare that a measure of music can be read as a word, music braille can be easily distinguished from literary braille.

Note Names and Rhythmic Values

In most cases a single braille cell gives both the name of a note and its rhythmic value. The upper dots of the cell—1, 2, 4, and 5—are used to form the name of the note, and the lower dots—3 and 6—determine the rhythmic value of that note. The seven note names beginning with C are written in the upper part of the cell:

⠩ ⠑ ⠋ ⠛ ⠓ ⠊ ⠚

A unique feature of braille music is that each rhythmic value has two possible meanings. For example, a quarter note is formed by adding dot 6 to any of the characters above, and a 64th note is also formed by adding dot 6. The performer must determine the rhythmic value intended by counting the beats in each measure. For complex situations there is a distinction-of-value sign, which is rarely needed. The following table shows the notes with rhythmic values.

Letter name	C	D	E	F	G	A	B
Whole or 16th:	⠿	⠵	⠯	⠷	⠾	⠮	⠽
Half or 32nd:							
Quarter or 64th:							
Eighth or 128th:							

There are braille signs for rests, of course, and for dotted or double dotted notes. When a note appears with an accidental, the accidental precedes the note, and the following signs are used:

sharp ⠩   double sharp ⠩⠩

flat ⠣   double flat ⠣⠣

natural ⠡

Headings

Tempo indications, metronome markings, key signatures, and time or meter signatures are given in that order in a heading at the beginning of each piece or movement. Words that indicate the movement, mood, or tempo are written in literary braille.

Metronome markings generally consist of a note value, an equal sign (dots 2-3-5-6), and either a number or another note value. Since the note C is used in braille to represent a note of indeterminant pitch, all metronome markings contain a C with the appropriate rhythmic value dots. The first metronome marking below reads, "A quarter note equals 72." The second reads, "A dotted eighth note equals an eighth note."

If there is another metronome marking during the piece, it appears in the body of the music preceded and followed by a space.

Key signatures show only the number of sharps or flats, since they cannot be placed on a staff to show pitches as in print. Time signatures that contain numbers are shown as an upper-cell number (utilizing dots 1-2-4-5) followed by a lower-cell number (utilizing dots 2-3-5-6). Key and time signatures are usually combined. The following are representative key and time signatures.

In braille edition pages 211 and 212

⠩⠀⠩⠀⠩⠀⠩ One sharp, four-four time

⠣⠀⠣⠀⠩⠀⠩⠀⠩ Two flats, three-eight time

⠩⠩⠀⠩⠩⠀⠩⠩⠀⠩⠩⠀⠩⠩ Three sharps, "C" or common time

⠩⠀⠩⠀⠩⠀⠩⠀⠩ Four flats, cut time

⠩⠀⠩⠀⠩⠀⠩⠀⠩⠀⠩ Five sharps, two-four time

A change of key signature, time signature, or both may appear in the music. If so, it will be preceded and followed by a space.

Determining Octave Locations of Notes

Pitches are indicated by letter name and octave. The octaves are numbered from one to seven beginning with the lowest C on the piano keyboard. For example, all of the notes in the lowest complete octave of the piano beginning with C and going up through the next B above are notes in the first octave. Each octave has a sign that immediately precedes the note it affects; no other sign may come between the octave sign and the note, not even an accidental. The following are the octave signs beginning with first octave, each preceding a quarter note C.

⠈⠩ ⠘⠩ ⠸⠩ ⠐⠩ ⠨⠩ ⠰⠩ ⠠⠩

Notes lower than first octave: ⠠⠠ ⠐⠠ ⠸⠠

Notes higher than seventh octave: ⠠⠂ ⠐⠂ ⠸⠂

Whenever a note has an octave sign, the pitch is clearly identified. When there is no sign, the octave location of a note is determined by the melodic interval between that note and the one that immediately precedes it. The basic rules for octave signs have remained constant throughout the history of the music code. This explanation from *Musical Notation for the Blind*, British and Foreign Blind, Assoc., London, 1889, is still valid.

"The first note in a piece of music, or a main part of it, must always be preceded by its octave mark. For the succeeding notes the following rules apply: If the next note forms an ascending or descending second or third; it does not receive an octave mark, even if it is not in the same octave as the marked note. If it forms an ascending or descending fourth or fifth, it only receives an octave mark if it is not in the same octave as the first marked note. A note which is placed at an interval of a sixth or more from the marked note always receives an octave mark."

The melody to "My Bonnie Lies over the Ocean" will illustrate these rules.

Example:

In braille edition pages 213 and 214

After the time signature, given in the first three cells, the piece starts with an octave sign. The second note has an octave sign because it is a sixth from the first note. Since each succeeding note is an ascending or descending second or third, no more octave signs appear in the phrase even though the melody moves down into the third octave. At the chorus, "Bring back, bring back...," the melody moves in fourths as follows:

Example:

The fourths do not have octave signs because they stay in the same octave; other intervals do not require octave signs.

Some transcriptions employ octave signs more frequently (such as piano music with octave signs at the beginning of each measure), but these rules apply whenever an octave sign does not precede a note.

In-accords

In-accords are signs used to link together contrapuntal voices or parts that belong to one measure and that, in most instances, are performed simultaneously. In print, two or more voices can be aligned vertically; in braille each voice must be written horizontally.

As its name implies, the full-measure in-accord  links two parts, each containing a full measure of rhythmic value.

Example:

In the above example the upper voice consists of an octave sign and two half notes (first through third cells) and the lower voice, an octave sign and four quarter notes (sixth through tenth cells). The two voices are connected by an in-accord sign (fourth and fifth cells).

A part-measure in-accord sign ⠠⠐⠒ links two parts of equal rhythmic value less than a full measure in duration; the section sign ⠘⠦⠰⠴ indicates the beginning or end of the part-measure in-accord. There may be more than one part-measure in-accord in a measure, and a part-measure in-accord may be combined with a full measure in-accord as in the following example.

Example:

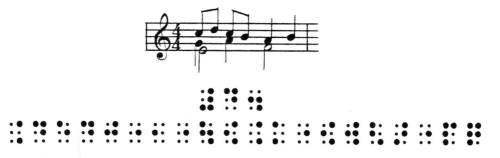

In braille edition pages 216 and 217

The first four eighth notes are to be played in-accord with quarter notes G and A. The section sign following those two quarter notes separates the part-measure in-accord from quarter notes A and B. The full-measure in-accord sign indicates that all of the previous material is to be played with two half notes that follow. Altogether, these signs comprise one measure of music.

The performance of in-accords depends somewhat on whether they occur in keyboard, instrumental, or vocal music. In keyboard and string music all parts linked by in-accord sign(s) are played simultaneously, unless there is a small-type sign or a word such as *ossia* indicating optional notes. In music for wind instruments and in some percussion music, in-accords indicate a choice of notes or present music for separate instruments (for example, clarinets 1 and 2). In other percussion music (for example, xylophone), the parts are played simultaneously. In solo vocal music, in-accords present a variation of notes for different verses or languages as well as a choice of notes. In choral music, in-accords are also used for divided parts.

Although in-accords join parts of the same measure, each part is read independently. Accidentals, doublings, and repeats before an in-accord sign do not affect music after that in-accord sign. Doublings are carried over to the next measure, where they affect only the corresponding section. When the only sign preceding or following an in-accord sign is a repeat, the corresponding part of the preceding measure should be repeated. In most post-1929 transcriptions, an octave sign appears after each in-accord sign. When no octave sign follows an in-accord sign, the pitch of the next note is determined by the last note in the corresponding section of the preceding measure.

Intervals and Chords

A chord is written by naming the pitch of either the top or bottom note and showing the remaining notes as intervals from that note. The following signs are for intervals of a second through an octave.

Example: ⠦ ⠼ ⠴ ⠳ ⠒ ⠲ ⠱

A chord may be read either up or down from the written note. The chord ⠩⠌⠱ is read, "C, third interval, fifth interval." Reading up, this represents the notes C E G; reading down, it represents the notes C A F. In instrumental music, harmonic intervals are generally written up for instruments of lower range such as cello and double bass and down for treble instruments such as violin and guitar. Harmonic intervals in choral music are generally written up in men's voice parts and down in women's voice parts; exceptions sometimes occur. In keyboard music the pedal and left hand parts are written up almost without exception, but the intervals for the right hand may be written in either direction. In some compositions a transcriber's note specifies the direction of the intervals; in the absence of transcriber's note, examine in-accords and fingering.

In braille edition pages 218-220

In-accords are usually written in the same direction as the intervals of the part in which they occur. If notes before an in-accord sign are higher in pitch than notes following that sign, chords in that same part should read down throughout the transcription. If notes before an in-accord are lower, chords should read up.

Fingering may be another clue to the direction of intervals. In a right hand part the chord ⠿⠿⠿⠿⠿ reads "fifth octave, whole note C, first finger, third interval, fifth interval." Since C is played with the first finger (thumb), the third and fifth intervals must be above C. The chord ⠿⠿⠿⠿⠿ is the same, except that the fingering sign indicates fifth finger. The third and fifth intervals must be below C.

The following statements apply to all chords regardless of whether they read up or down.

1. Each interval is calculated from the written note.

2. Each successive interval is farther from the written note.

Statements 1 and 2 are illustrated in the following chord.

Example: (read up) ⠿⠿⠿⠿⠿

The chord is read "third octave, whole note C, fifth, third, octave," representing third octave C, third octave G, fourth octave E, and fifth octave C.

3. An interval between two adjacent notes is not greater than an octave unless specified by an octave sign. The chord ⠿⠿⠿⠿ is a tenth (third octave C with fourth octave third, i.e., E).

4. An octave sign is used to indicate a prime or unison. Example: ⠿ ⠿ ⠿ ⠿

(fourth octave C, fourth octave, octave interval.)

5. Intervals may be modified by accidentals. Example: ⠿ ⠿ ⠿ ⠿ (C, flat, third, fifth.)

6. A slur following a chord applies to the entire chord.

7. A chord tie ⠿ ⠿ indicates that at least two members of the chord are tied over to the next chord.

Example: (read down) ⠿ ⠿ ⠿ ⠿ ⠿ ⠿ ⠿ ⠿ ⠿

(fifth octave, C A E, chord tie, C A F.)

The notes C and A are tied while E of the first chord moves to F of the second chord.

8. The tie sign ⠿ ⠿ affects only one member of a chord, the note or interval that immediately precedes it.

Example: (read down) ⠿ ⠿ ⠿ ⠿ ⠿ ⠿ ⠿ ⠿ ⠿

(fifth octave, C A tie E, C A F.)

A is tied, E moves to F, and C is sounded again.

These basic principles of interval and chord-reading apply to formats in current use. Exceptions that occasionally occur in other formats are discussed in the section, "Formats for Braille Music."

Repeats

Many more repeats are used in braille music than in print because they facilitate reading and memorization. The most common repeat sign is ⠿ . When preceded and followed by a space, this sign means to repeat the preceding measure. If the same sign appears within a measure, it becomes a part-measure repeat; enough of the music immediately preceding the sign is repeated to complete the required number of beats.

Repetition of a specific measure or group of measures is indicated by a numeral sign followed by the single measure number or the inclusive numbers to be repeated. These numbers are given in the lower-cell position utilizing dots 2-3-5-6. A number sign followed by a number in the regular upper-cell position also indicates repetition. If an upper or lower-cell numeral is preceded by a space, examine the representative entries on pages 50 to 57 to find the exact meaning intended.

Doubling

Doubling is the braille device that allows a sign to remain in effect without constantly being repeated. In literary braille, doubling is used for italics, and in music braille it is used for many different signs. There is no parallel practice in print music.

A sign is doubled when it appears twice in succession, indicating at least four repetitions of that particular feature of the music. Occasionally a sign is redoubled. A doubled or redoubled sign remains in effect until cancelled by the single form of the sign.

The sign appears in its normal position in relation to the note when doubled and when marking the end of a series. For example, a staccato sign ⠠⠄ affects the note that follows it, an interval sign affects the note that precedes it, and a simple slur ⠠⠅ comes between notes. In the following example, notice that these positions are retained at the beginning and at the end of each doubling.

Example:

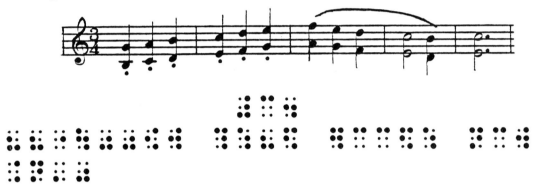

The first six notes are staccato, the next five notes are slurred, and every note forms a two-note chord with intervals of a sixth below.

Doubling that precedes an in-accord sign has no effect on the music following an in-accord sign. Instead, the doubling carries over to the corresponding section of the following measure.

Doubling continues through the single-cell repeat sign ⠶ . When a repeat contains a number sign, however, such as ⠶⠂ (repeat four bars) or ⠼⠁⠼⠓ (repeat measures one through eight), a sign must be redoubled after the repeated measures. *Segnos, da capos,* and double bars terminate doubling.

In braille edition pages 224 and 225

A doubled interval sign may be preceded by an accidental which applies only to the initial occurrence of the interval. Since an accidental may not be doubled, it does not affect the remaining intervals in the doubled passage.

Example: (read down)

⠀⠀⠀⠀⠀⠀⠀⠀⠀⠀⠀

Fifth octave E is played with C-sharp. The third interval sign is doubled, so F-sharp is played with D, and G-sharp is played with E. (The doubled intervals are not sharped.) At the beginning of the second measure, the third interval is again sharped (C-sharp). Since it is also redoubled, the remaining notes are played with thirds. The final sign shows the end of the doubled passage.

The octave interval sign is an exception to the rule. The doubled octave interval sign means that perfect octaves are formed. If the written note has an accidental, the octave has the same accidental.

Example:

⠀⠀⠀⠀⠀⠀⠀⠀⠀⠀⠀

Each note is played with an octave interval and every note is a sharp.

Grouping

Grouping is a method of combining 16th, 32nd, or 64th notes into units of a beat or a natural division of a beat. Its purpose is to facilitate reading of braille pitches written in the upper part of the cell and to provide easier recognition of beats or beat divisions.

Grouping consists of writing only the first note of a unit with its true rhythmic value and the remaining notes as letter names. Since notes without dots 3 or 6 are normally eighth notes, the grouping device is never used before an eighth note or an eighth rest.

A rest may be the first member of a group, but if the rest occurs later in the unit, the grouping device is not used. In the following example, the sign ⠐ is a 16th rest.

Example:

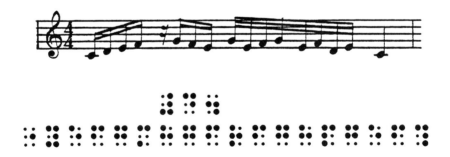

The first beat is four 16th notes; the second beat is a 16th rest and three 16th notes; the third beat is eight 32nd notes in two half-beat groups; and the fourth beat is a quarter note.

Chords may be grouped following the same rules, and other signs may appear between the notes without affecting

In braille edition pages 227 and 228

the grouping. In the following example, the sign ⠰⠆⠰⠆ indicates the beginning of a *crescendo*.

Example: (read intervals down)

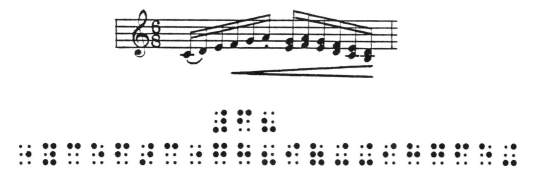

The one-measure example in six-eight time contains twelve 16th notes grouped into two beats of six notes each. The signs for slur, *crescendo,* staccato, and the doubled interval of a third do not affect the grouping.

Correlation of Words with Melody

In print, the correlation of music and text is shown by vertical alignment. In braille there is no spatial correlation; in some formats the text is even in a different paragraph from the music.

In braille vocal music, each syllable is understood to be sung to a single note of music unless a braille sign indicates to the contrary. The syllabic slur ⠒⠒ in the music line indicates that more than one note goes with a single syllable; this slur, which may be doubled if necessary, connects all notes to be sung on one syllable.

In braille edition pages 228 and 229   179

Quotation marks in the text line indicate that more than one syllable is sung on a single note. They surround the syllables that are to be elided (sung together), and in some transcriptions the corresponding note is followed by a sign for two ⠆⠆ or three ⠒⠒ to indicate the number of syllables falling on that note.

Example:

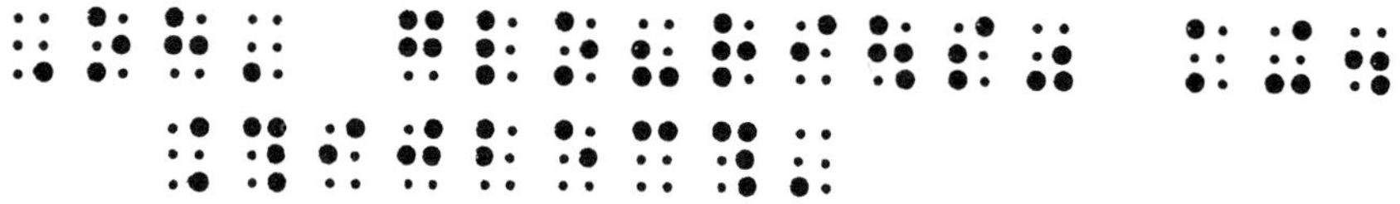

⠠⠦⠔� (braille music line)

The text "Oh, glorious king" is written in the top line and the music is in the next line. "Oh" is sung on fifth octave C, "glo-" on eighth note A. Quotation marks surround "ri-ous" indicating that the two syllables are sung together on eighth note B which is followed by the sign ⠆⠆ to confirm that two syllables go with that note. The one syllable word "king" is sung on the last two notes which are slurred together.

A much less common system of correlating text with melody is found primarily in early liturgical music. It uses hyphens instead of slurs in the music line; see chant notation, page 144.

Contemporary Resources for Braille Music Notation

The following resources are available in print and in braille. All except the first book may be purchased from American Printing House for the Blind, Louisville, KY 40206.

In braille edition pages 229-231

Krolick, Bettye. *How To Read Braille Music, Book I.* Explanation of how to read instrumental, keyboard, and vocal music at the beginning stages; written at a fifth grade reading level. Braille edition: NBA Braille Book Bank, 422 Clinton Ave. S., Rochester, NY 14620. Print edition: Stipes Publishing Co., 10-12 Chester St., Champaign, IL 61820.

Jenkins, Edward. *Primer of Braille Music, New Revised Edition.* Reading lessons with fewer explanations and more examples than the above.

De Garmo, Mary. *Introduction to Braille Music Transcription.* A textbook on transcribing print music into braille; used in conjunction with the following code manual.

Spanner, H.V., comp. *Revised International Manual of Braille Music Notation 1956* and *1975 American Addendum.* Code manual of braille music in the United States. For the music transcriber and for the advanced reader who needs detailed information about the music code.

SELECTIVE BIBLIOGRAPHY

Books and periodicals included in this bibliography are in print or braille or both formats, as indicated.

When titles are at the Library of Congress, no other locations are given although copies may often be found elsewhere. Titles not at the Library of Congress are with the author or at the Perkins School for the Blind.

For further information about sources, write to the following addresses.

Library of Congress	Music Section
	National Library Service for the Blind and Physically Handicapped
	Library of Congress
	Washington, D.C. 20542
Author	Bettye Krolick
	602 Ventura Road
	Champaign, Illinois 61820
Perkins	Samuel P. Hayes Research Library
	Perkins School for the Blind
	175 North Beacon Street
	Watertown, Massachusetts 02172

Braille, Louis. *Procédé pour Ecrire les Paroles, la Musique et le Plain-Chant au Moyen de Points*. Paris: Institution Royale des Jeunes Aveugles, 1829.

Perkins; print

Braille Music Notation. Conforming with the decisions of the International Congress convoked by American Braille Press Inc., Paris, April 1929. Edited with footnotes showing preferred American practices. Paris: American Braille Press, 1930.

Library of Congress; print, braille
The braille edition, published by the American Printing House for the Blind in 1951, shows practices preferred at the American Printing House.

Decaux, Etienne. *Le Braille dans les Langues Slaves*. Paris: Institut d'Etudes Slaves de l'Université de Paris, 1956.

Library of Congress; print

De Garmo, Mary Turner, *Introduction to Braille Music Transcription*. Washington: Library of Congress, 1970.

Library of Congress; print, braille

Dictionary of Braille Contractions. London: British and Foreign Blind Association, 1895.

Perkins; print

Gaudet, Par J. *Les Aveugles Musiciens.* Paris: Fain Thunot, 1846.

Perkins; print

Goupil, L'Abbé. "Nouvelle Notation Musicale Tangible à l'Usage des Aveugles." In *Sonnets et Poésies Diverses.* Tours: Deslis, 1892.

Perkins; print

Hayashi, Shigeo. *International Manual of Braille Music Notation.* Tokyo: Nippon Cultural Center, 1972.

Author; print

Internationales Punkt-Musikschrift-System nach den Ergebnissen der Pariser Verhandlungen im April 1929. Hannover-Kirchrode: Verein zur Förderung der Blindenbildung, 1931.

Library of Congress; print
Describes German practices.
184

Japan Braille Council. *Braille Notation for Japanese Music.* Kyoto: Kyoto Professional School for the Blind, 1955.

Perkins; print

A Key to the Braille Alphabet and Musical Notation. London: British and Foreign Blind Association, 1871.

Perkins; print

Musical Notation for the Blind, Braille System. As arranged by the International Commission, and confirmed by the Congress of Cologne, 1888. rev. ed. London: British and Foreign Blind Association, 1900.

Library of Congress; print

Musical Notation for the Blind, Braille System. London: British and Foreign Blind Association, 1889.

Perkins; print

Nemeth, Abraham. *Dictionary of Braille Musical Symbols.* Louisville: American Printing House for the Blind, 1953.

Library of Congress; braille

Notation Musicale Braille. Conforme aux Décisions du Congrès International convoqué par American Braille Press Inc., à Paris, en Avril 1929. Paris: American Braille Press, 1930.

Library of Congress; print
Describes French practices.

Riedinger. "Notenschrift für Blinde." *Allgemeine Musikalische Zeitung* 57 (1810): 907-920.

Library of Congress; print

Reuss, Alexander. *Development and Problems of Musical Notation for the Blind.* Translated by Ellen Kerney and Merle E. Frampton. New York: New York Institute for the Education of the Blind, 1935.

Library of Congress; print

Reuss, Alexander. *Index à la Notation Musicale Braille.* Leipzig: Deutsche Zentralbücherei für Blinde, 1966.

Author; braille
French edition of *Lehrbuch de Welt-Blindennotenschrift.*

Reuss, Alexander. *Lehrbuch der Welt-Blindennotenschrift.* Leipzig: Deutsche Zentralbücherei für Blinde, 1964.

Author; braille

Roblin, Jean. *The Reading Fingers: Life of Louis Braille, 1809-1852.* Translated by Ruth G. Mandalian. New York: American Foundation for the Blind, 1955.

Library of Congress; print

Robyn, Henry. *Thorough Description of the Braille System for the Reading and Writing of Music.* St. Louis: August Wiebusch & Son, 1867.

Library of Congress; print

Rodenberg, L. W. *Key to Braille Music Notation.* Louisville, Ky.: American Printing House for the Blind, 1925.

Library of Congress; print, braille

Spanner, H. V., comp. *Revised International Manual of Braille Music Notation 1956.* Part I: *Western Music.* Based on decisions reached at the International Conference on Braille Music, Paris, 1954. With corrections authorized by World Braille Council, September, 1961.

American ed. Louisville, Ky.: American Printing House for the Blind, 1961.

Library of Congress; print, braille

Tabela de Sinais para Violão (Guitarra). São Paulo: Fundação para o Livro do Cego no Brasil, 1961.

Author; print

Watson, Edward. Foreword to *Braille Music Notation*. Paris: American Braille Press, 1930.

INDEX

This index covers terms, subjects, and proper names found in the sections on history, formats, and fundamentals of braille music. Individual braille signs are not covered. For these, the reader is referred to the contents, where braille signs are listed in standard order.

196

☆ U. S. GOVERNMENT PRINTING OFFICE : 1979 O - 299-000